THE
HARRIS FREE PUBLIC LIBRARY
AND MUSEUM, PRESTON
1893–1993

by

John Convey

Lancashire County Books, 1993

To Bruce.

God gave him such a love for history and the gift to communicate its delights to all who knew him.

The Harris Free Public Library and Museum,Preston, 1893–1993
by John Convey

Text copyright © John Convey, 1993

Published by Lancashire County Books, 143 Corporation Street, Preston, 1993.

Typeset by Carnegie Publishing Ltd., 18 Maynard Street, Preston.

Printed by T. Snape & Co., Preston.

British Library Cataloguing-in-Publication Data
A CIP record for this book is available from the British Library.

ISBN 1-871236-30-4

ACKNOWLEDGEMENTS

I WOULD LIKE TO THANK: Alex Walker and her staff in the Harris Museum and Art Gallery for their assistance and advice; my colleagues in the Reference Library, particularly Terry Shaw and Ann Dennison for helping with sources and for reading through the script; the Attendants in the Harris for their assistance and patience, particularly when I was attempting photography; the staff at the Lancashire Record Office; the staff of Citibank Life for allowing me to photograph the building from Crystal House; and particularly Zoë Lawson, of Lancashire County Books, for invaluable advice and assistance.

John Convey,
Southport,
August 1993

CONTENTS

A FREE LIBRARY AND MUSEUM FOR PRESTON?—AYE, EVENTUALLY!

MANY PEOPLE HAVE CONTRIBUTED to the library and museum life of Preston and its neighbourhood over the last hundred years—Victorian men who pursued the goal of establishing a free library and museum, those in office who adopted the Acts of Parliament, those who planned, financed and built the Harris Free Public Library and Museum and those whose responsibility has been to govern it over the years, and the staff who have provided services, and most of all the people who use the services provided—from Preston, Lancashire, the United Kingdom and indeed from far-flung lands of the world. The services provide not only for leisure and entertainment, but also for information to aid research in education, industry, commerce, public services, health and in many other areas of modern-day living.

Entering the Harris building today, the visitor is struck by the contrasting features living side by side—computers recording the return of books to the library with priceless centuries-old books from the Dr Shepherd Library; continuously playing video recordings showing Preston's history and life with the frieze of King Ashur-Nasir-Pal II of the ninth century BC; finding information instantly from a computer in California in a room boasting four white columns of the Ionic Order of ancient Greek architecture; and a modern cafe tastefully interwoven among the grecian columns of the ground floor.

For all its size, the Harris building has long since been unable to provide all the library and museum services required by the community from this one building and has reached out to people through several permanent branch libraries, prison libraries, services to people in homes for the elderly or at home, and library and museum services to schools. There are now 94,614 registered library readers in the Preston district, borrowing nearly 1½ million books a year—833,335 of these from the Harris building itself. About 180,000 people visit the museum and art gallery each year; in Guild year, 1992, this figure was well over 200,000. If the founding fathers could see their creation today, no doubt they would congratulate themselves on how the services have developed, if a little nonplussed by the presence of such items as computers, compact discs for music and text, records, videos, fax and photocopying machines, telephones and all the other modern technology which is such a part of the library and museum world of today.

The Public Libraries Act of 1850 allowed councils to levy a ½d. rate for the establishment and maintenance of a museum and/or library; under an earlier Museum Act of 1845 nearby Warrington had established a combined museum and library, the town clerk explaining, 'we have a skilled naturalist who is competent to stuff and prepare specimens and he and his family act also as librarians'.[1] The circumstances were improved in 1855 when councils were empowered to levy a 1d. rate to purchase books, newspapers, maps and specimens; and the adoption of the Act could be decided by a two-thirds majority at a public meeting of ratepayers; by 1877 this had changed to a majority of a poll or a public meeting. In 1854, Preston had begun the process towards adopting the Act; several meetings were held, both by the 'industrial classes' and the wealthier, more influential members of the community. Some of the 'gentlemen' on the 'general committee' for establishing a public free library and museum in Preston included Revd Robert Harris, Charles Roger Jacson, William Dobson, Revd Charles Harrison Wood, and a certain Edmund Robert Harris; these were to figure greatly in the story about to unfold, as was the working men's committee, the secretary of which was Thomas Edelston, who was destined to be mayor in 1893, the year that the Harris Free Public Library and Museum was officially opened. This committee held fund-raising events, such as soirees, excursions and lectures, as well as encouraging working people in the mills to subscribe to the fund for establishing a library. By the end of 1857, the working men's fund had reached £476 4s. 6d., and the general committee's fund about £1,800—some of these donations were conditional and may have been only promises.

With regard to the library, a distinction was made between the lending department and the reference department from the beginning; the publication *A Free Library and Museum for Preston: Aye or No* said that every well-constituted free library had a part for reference, for those who have made some progress in the art of self-improvement, and a part for lending, with the hope that this may reach to every fireside.[2] There were libraries already in existence in the town, such as those in the Mechanics' Institute, the Law Library and the Dr Shepherd Library; there were also a number of lending libraries in mills and schools in the town; but it was not thought that a new free library would have an adverse effect on these. The general feeling was that a public library would benefit all classes of people, and would enhance the reputation of the town. It was hoped that accommodation might be provided in the new town hall—the foundation stone of this was laid in 1862 and it was opened officially on 3 October 1867—but this was not to be, yet. The initial enthusiasm generated in the years 1854 to 1859 seemed to ebb, and the movement for adopting the Public Libraries Act in Preston was postponed for nearly twenty years.

The developments in education, particularly the passing of the Education Act in 1870 with its provisions for universal elementary education, acted as a spur to councils to adopt the Free Libraries Acts. It is no surprise, therefore, that at the Preston Borough Council meeting of the 27 September 1877, it was decided to appoint a committee to 'consider the propriety of establishing a free library in Preston'.³ The committee comprised many names which had been and would be for many years associated with the public library and museum movement in the town, such as Alderman Edmund Birley, Charles Roger Jacson, Thomas Edelston, James Hibbert and William Gilbertson. This resolution was further developed and agreed at the next meeting on the 25 October in the same year, when a special committee was to consider whether to establish a free library and museum, and if so, whether the Dr Shepherd Library should be part of it, and whether the books and objects belonging to the Literary and Philosophical Institution should be purchased, and to establish whether any money raised in the 1850s was still in existence.

Money from existing funds was handed over—£395 12s. 1d. from the working-class movement and £205 7s. 5d. from the general fund; it is not clear what happened to the rest of the money that was collected in the 1850s. At a meeting on New Year's Day 1878, the council agreed to call a public meeting of the burgesses of the borough in accordance with the Public Libraries Act to decide whether to adopt the Act; at this meeting there was the first mention in the council of the connection of Edmund Robert Harris with the establishment of a library and museum; this gentleman had died in the previous year leaving a large amount of money and a detailed will indicating that a substantial proportion of his estate be used to establish one or more public institutions, including a free library. At the end of the month the council agreed to accept the offer of the Literary and Philosophical Institution to transfer their books, apparatus, philosophical instruments and other effects to the council for public use, and the council would pay the Institution £150. The Literary and Philosophical Society was established in October 1840, and the Cross Street building was opened on 9 December 1846; later this building was handed to the corporation and in 1880 it became home for the first public museum in the town. A public meeting of ratepayers was held on Tuesday 29 January 1878 in the guild hall; there was but a small audience present when the meeting was due to commence, but gradually the hall began to fill. There was some, mainly lighthearted, opposition to the proposal, but the motion was carried with only three votes against; speakers felt that the passing of the Education Act in 1870 was a particularly important reason for implementing the Acts. Shortly afterwards moves were begun to make use of a room in the town hall for a free public reading room and lending library, the room being occupied at that time by the exchange newsroom committee. In October of that year the members of the library committee were appointed the 'free public library committee', with the following purposes:

1   to carry out the Public Acts enabling town councils to establish public libraries and museums, and the several Acts amending the same, so far as applicable
2   to manage and transact all matters and purposes relating to the control and management of a free library and the officers and servants
3   to receive and arrange and to take all other necessary proceedings with respect to any articles included in any presentation, gift or bequest to the corporation for the library and museum
4   to examine and certify for payment all accounts relating to matters within the province of the committee.

The honour of being appointed the first librarian of the new free public library went to William Bramhall, who was paid £130 *per annum*, and was required to treat the job as full-time.

When the free public library finally opened its doors to the public on 1 January 1879, nearly twenty-five years had elapsed since the first moves were made to establish a free library. There was no ceremony at the opening—William Bramhall simply turned the key and let the public in! It was estimated that at least fifteen hundred people visited the library on the first day; there were seven hundred applications received for membership; and the room was described as 'one of the noblest rooms in the country'. By the time the Harris building was opened this room in the town hall was being described as 'the crowded, stuffy place in the Town Hall'!

The rules drawn up for the library make interesting reading today; some of them have long since been lost in the mists of time: no conversation was permitted; the lending library was open until 9.00 p.m. and the news and reading room until 10.00 p.m.; to be entitled to borrow books a person had to obtain the

The first chief librarian of the Harris Free Public Library, William Bramwell, in his office. He retired in 1916 at the age of eighty-one

signature of a burgess of Preston, who presumably took this responsibility seriously as he agreed to 'undertake to replace any book which shall be lost or materially damaged' by the borrower; if a library card were lost, it could be replaced for 1d; borrowers were allowed only one book out on loan at any time; anyone maliciously destroying or damaging anything in a library 'shall be guilty of a misdemeanour, and being duly convicted thereof, shall be liable to be imprisoned for any period not exceeding six months, and if a male, may during the period of such imprisonment be put to hard labour, or be once, twice or thrice privately whipped in such a manner as the Court before which a person shall be tried shall direct'.[4]

In August 1879 William Bramhall resigned as librarian and was succeeded by William Bramwell at a reduced salary of £2 per week. He had an assistant, William Sumner who earned the princely sum of fifteen shillings per week at this time. William Storey Bramwell was christened at St John's Church in Preston on 5 February 1835 and married Ellen Watson in April 1854; his father was a rope-maker. He was a contemporary at school of James Hibbert, who was later to be architect of the Harris Free Public Library and Museum. In 1860 he took charge of the Literary and Philosophical Institution in Cross Street, which included the Dr Shepherd Library and a museum. He was chief librarian at the free public library and museum until his retirement in February 1916; he died on Sunday 21 March 1917, at the age of eighty-two. The *Preston Guardian* states that William Bramwell devoted his whole time to the welfare of the library and to the encouragement of literary pursuits; he had a phenomenal memory and a fine talent for organisation.

For the next fifteen years, while the library was located in the town hall, the usage of the library increased year by year; by the time the Harris Free Public Library and Museum was opened to the public on 1 January 1894, the number of readers' tickets in use was over 19,000; this had risen from a total of 3,600 when the library opened in 1879; in the same period, the number of books issued per year had doubled, from 55,481 to 110,319.

In the early years books were classified under seven headings:

I   General History, Biography, Geography, Antiquities and Travels
II   Philology, Rhetoric, Logic, Mathematics, Physics, Natural History, Fine and Industrial Arts
III   Theology and Mental Philosophy
IV   Jurisprudence, Politics and Trade
V   Poetry and Drama
VI   Prose Fiction
VII Critical and Miscellaneous Works, Periodicals, Dictionaries, Encyclopedias, Reports, Translations from the Classics.

A catalogue of the holdings of the lending library was printed as early as 1880, and was arranged in the order of authors' names, with a simple shelf mark, including the first initial of the author's name, followed by one of the following letters denoting the size of the book: 'F' for folio (very large), 'Q' for quarto (large), 'O' for Octavo (medium), 'D' for Duodecimo (small); this letter would then be followed by a number—a sample entry being:

Baines, Edward. *History of Lancashire* 4 vols   1836   B Q 5

It is perhaps surprising to see the broad range of publications available for consultation in the reading room at the time, such as: the Army List, *Quarterly Review*, Registrar-General's Reports, Bradshaw's *Railway Guide*, *Contemporary Review*, *Economist*, *Builder*, *Spectator*, *Preston Herald*, *Preston Pilot*, *Liverpool and Southport Daily News*, *Daily Telegraph*, *The Times* and *Manchester Guardian*, among many others; many of these have been held continuously up to the present day.

The museum in Cross Street opened on the 1 May 1880, and was open from 11 a.m. until dusk. On the 29 April 1880 Miss Margaret Barton had been appointed curator of the museum at ten shillings per week; she held this post until her death in March 1891—the committee commented upon the 'diligent, faithful and satisfactory performance' of her duties; she was succeeded as curator by Thomas Busfield. In the years prior to its move to the new Harris building, the museum was attracting around twenty thousand visitors a year. The Revd Jonathan Shortt, the vicar of Hoghton, was appointed honorary curator of the museum in May 1882. He was a remarkably learned man who was said to have a profound and intimate knowledge of a few fields of scientific research, and an average acquaintance with the rest! He became vicar of Hoghton in 1853, where he remained until his death on 17 May 1899. When the museum was at Cross Street, he arranged and labelled the geological specimens and fossils. Later he became honorary curator of the Harris Museum, and was responsible for the beautiful and instructive arrangement of the natural history section of the Harris.[5] He also helped with the coin collection, and gave talks on the Assyrian and Greek friezes in the Harris building.

In December 1883, the corporation received a letter from the executors of the will of the late Richard Newsham, who had lived at No. 1 Winckley Square and been a justice of the peace, bequeathing paintings, drawings, miniatures and other art treasures to the corporation; it was thought that these could provide the nucleus of a fine arts collection. Until the completion of the Harris building, the construction of which had begun in October 1883, it was decided to locate the Newsham collection in part of the guild hall, underneath the south gallery. James Hibbert supervised the removal, the arrangement and the hanging of the pictures in the guild hall, and the gallery was opened for public viewing in May 1884. Richard Newsham was born in 1798, and was educated at Preston Grammar School under the Revd Robert Harris; he became a solicitor and from 1842 a justice of the peace, and professionally at least must have been well acquainted with Edmund Robert Harris. His bequest included sixty-two oil paintings and forty-five water-colours, including important British artists of the early Victorian period. Shortly before his death, he prepared a catalogue of his pictures and drawings. Richard Newsham visited the Royal Academy exhibition each year from 1820 to 1870. Among some of the other donations received in the early years was a copy of the general printed catalogue from the British Museum.

In March 1887 the library purchased what has proved to be a most useful work—422 volumes of the Hansard Parliamentary Debates which, including Cobbett's *Parliamentary History*, cover the years from 1066 onwards; the library has continued to hold an unbroken sequence of these debates; there was also the addition of 152 Ordnance Survey maps covering the county of Lancaster. An interesting donation was received from Charles Lilley, who had been on the general committee requesting the adoption of the Free Libraries Act in 1854. He had moved to Australia, and his donation was a three volume work—a *Pictorial and Descriptive Atlas of Australasia*, which includes over eight hundred engravings. In May 1889 the executors of the will of John Dewhurst, of Ribblesdale Place, donated prints and pictures to the 'Free Library of the Borough of Preston'; by this time the number of titles in the library was well over sixteen thousand.

The library and museum were going from strength to strength, but the lack of space and purpose-built accommodation was becoming ever more apparent. It was with growing anticipation that the people of Preston watched a splendid new building rising throughout the 1880s. At the end of 1888 the free library committee expressed the hope that this new building would soon be delivered up to the corporation. This scheme, coming to fruition at the east side of the market square, had been planned as far back as 1878. It owed its existence principally to a local man who had died in 1877 and in his will left money to be used for one or more public institutions, one of which could be a library; that man was Edmund Robert Harris, and it is to him that we now turn.

NOTES

1.   Kelly, T., *History of Public Libraries in Great Britain, 1845–1965* (Library Association, 1973), pp. 10–11.
2.   *A Free Library and Museum for Preston: Aye or No?* (Preston, 1854).
3.   Preston Borough Council Minutes, 1876–7.
4.   Preston Borough Council Minutes, 1878–9, pp. 38–9.
5.   *Preston Guardian*, 20 May 1899, p. 8.

EDMUND ROBERT HARRIS

EDMUND ROBERT HARRIS was born on the 6 September 1803 and was christened at St John's Parish Church, Preston on the second anniversary of his parents' wedding, 19 November 1803. He was the son of Robert and Nancy Harris; Robert Harris was the vicar of St George's Church in Preston, and also headmaster of the Free Grammar School, which at that time was in Stoneygate. He was headmaster from 1788 until 1835, during which time he lived in the school house which still exists—now known as Arkwright House.

Robert Harris came from Clitheroe, and was christened there on 4 March 1764; he was educated at Clitheroe Grammar School and the University of Cambridge. He was 'licensed to the perpetual Curacy and Chapel of Saint George in Preston' in December 1797, and was there until his death on the 6 January 1862, at the age of ninety-seven; he was buried in the churchyard of St George's; he was also chaplain to the Royal Preston Volunteers from July 1797 and in July 1805 he was made incumbent of the parish of Much Hoole, charged with the care of the souls and the parishioners of that parish, until 1812. He was respected and loved by his parishioners and his family. After his death, people well remembered the reverend and venerable old gentleman who, on the Christmas Day before he died, preached a sermon with all the fire and impressiveness of an old veteran who well knew that his earthly work was fast drawing to a close. Years later at the official opening of the Harris Free Public Library and Museum building, the mayor, Thomas Edelston, said that Robert Harris stood for toleration and charity, he was quiet and unpretentious. He abstained from everything likely to give offence to those whose religious views differed from his own; he was content to preach the gospel in simple but effective terms, to live the life he preached, to be at peace with his neighbours. He gained the sincere respect of all classes of the community and the affection of all who were intimately acquainted with him.

Robert Harris married a local girl, Nancy Lodge, and they had four children: Robert, Edmund Robert, Thomas and Ellen Elizabeth; Robert died in infancy

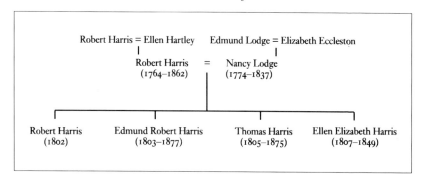

The Harris family tree.

in 1802, Thomas was born in 1805 and the boys' sister in 1807; none of them ever married. A contemporary, Charles Brown, said of Thomas, 'he was reputed at the Winckley Club to exercise great economy in the purchase of his cigars; they were said to be of a very inferior quality and he puffed into the billiard room rather an unpleasant aroma'. Of Ellen Elizabeth he said that a Mr John Cooper of The Oaks, Penwortham, was at one time 'matrimonially disposed' towards Miss Harris, but she did not encourage his advances because he could not ride on horseback! Ellen Elizabeth died in 1849, and in her memory and that of her mother and father, the brothers built a new chancel at St Andrew's Church in Ashton with a memorial window; there is a bust of Ellen Elizabeth by Rowland Rhodes in the Harris building today.

Edmund Robert spent his early years in the school house of the Free Grammar School; presumably he was educated in the school too. Years later in his will he was to ensure the continued connection of the Harris name with the grammar school by establishing scholarships for the benefit of pupils at the school; these scholarships amounted to £3,000. The school-house had been built in 1728, and was later to be made famous by Richard Arkwright who used a back room for the development of his spinning machine; the building has since seen a number of uses: a public house, an educational centre in the early 1980s, and now an office for the Age Concern charity. Edmund and Jonathan Lodge, brothers of Edmund Robert's mother, were solicitors in Chapel Street, and the brothers Harris were articled to the firm. When their uncles retired, the brothers were given the firm to run as partners. When Robert Harris retired from the headmastership of the grammar school, the family moved to 13 Ribblesdale Place.

Thomas Edelston, who was mayor at the official opening of the Harris Free Public Library and Museum in 1893, joined the Harrises' firm of solicitors in

'Whinfield', Ashton-upon-Ribble, where Edmund Robert Harris lived in the last few years of his life.

1844 and remained with them for twenty-two years. He described Edmund Robert as an able man, conscientious and upright, but incapable of taking part in any public business; he shrank from appearing ostentatious or prominent. Edmund Robert Harris succeeded John Forrest as the deputy prothonotary for Lancashire in 1848, a post which he held until 1865—a prothonotary was the chief clerk or registrar in the Court of Common Pleas for Lancaster. On John Forrest's death, the bizarre spectacle was seen of a number of local solicitors scurrying down to London to seek his appointment as prothonotary; Edmund Robert Harris was the successful applicant. In 1865 he became acting prothonotary and associate for Lancashire, and in 1869 prothonotary and associate; he held this office until his retirement in 1874.

Edmund Robert and Thomas moved to Whinfield in Ashton-upon-Ribble shortly after the death of their father, and lived in some style in this large residence which included several bedrooms and dressing rooms, dining room, drawing room, library, smoke room, as well as servants' quarters. It was pleasantly situated overlooking the river. After their deaths (Thomas had died in 1875), when, according to the will of Edmund Robert, all the household goods and furniture were auctioned, one of the items was a cellar of wines containing over two hundred dozen bottles of choice vintage wines!

In his later years, Edmund Robert suffered from bronchitis and other problems, including heart disease. He died on the 27 May 1877, and was buried at St Andrew's Churchyard in Ashton on Friday 1 June. A large number of people attended the funeral, despite the terrible drenching showers which fell throughout the morning. The funeral cortege left Whinfield shortly after eleven o'clock; the cortege included the vicar of St Andrew's and his assistant, tenants and servants walking in front of the hearse and six pairs on either side, the Revd Charles Harrison Wood, and prominent figures from the town. On Sunday 3 June, the Revd Wood preached a funeral sermon at St George's Church, which had long been associated with the name of Harris, as Revd Wood took over as vicar from Robert Harris in 1862. Revd Wood was shortly to become one of the trustees of the will of the deceased Edmund Robert Harris. In his funeral sermon, Revd Wood said that the character of the man he had to speak about was one of the most difficult with which he had ever had to deal. He was one of the most punctilious of men in matters of business and often appeared to an unbusinesslike mind to carry things with too fine a point, and that he was more than necessarily cautious. Everything must be done with strictness, propriety, exactness and integrity; everything must be moulded in the proper form, ever in strict accordance with the letter of the law. No work must be slighted, no trifles spared in the execution; it was doubtless this close attention to detail and its consequent security that gained for him that character of being so able and erudite a lawyer whose judgement was always to be depended upon and his advice so eagerly sought for and so promptly given. Had he taken up any other profession he would have missed his vocation. He was the ideal and the personification of a lawyer who could listen to every man's business and then keep his own to himself. His private character was much more difficult to understand than his public; Revd Wood was convinced that he had a keener perception, a fuller insight and a more just esteem of personal character than the outside world ever credited him with. His inner conscious life was folded up as it were, and however much they might try to open it up by genial warmth and social intercourse, they could only succeed in partly doing so. He was never what the world would call a front rank man in life. His aim and object was to do what he had to do well, humbly, quietly, without ostentation, preferring rather to walk in the secluded paths of life than tread the thoroughfares which led to fame and glory.[1] Later Charles Roger Jacson was to observe that Edmund Robert had 'filled a public office of great importance in the County and presented in his own person an example of the three objects for which the Harris Library and Museum was founded: literature, art and science; in literature he was familiar with Latin and modern languages, his art was music, his science the dignified science of law'.

Edmund Robert Harris was a very rich man. Being the last of the line of the Harrises, he had inherited wealth from his parents, from his uncles, his brother and his sister. He had investments in railway stocks and real estate, as well as the income derived from his professional occupation. He was a generous person both while he was alive and in the provisions of his will. He had intimated to Thomas Edelston before his death that the bulk of his fortune would be left for charitable purposes. While he was alive, when it became known that a ward for infectious diseases was needed at the infirmary, he immediately handed over £7,000 for the provision of this; many other donations were given anonymously. Those who knew him believed that he would never turn down a request for assistance, and often gave more than was requested. One of the provisions of his will was that trust monies should be used to 'establish or build and endow a convalescent hospital, or orphanage, or almshouses, or literary or scientific institution, or a free library, or all or any of them, or any other charitable institution or other institution of public utility which the trustees may think proper and which may contribute to perpetuate the remembrance of my father and his family in the town'.[2] By the time of the official opening of the Harris building in 1893, the amount of money spent from the Harris bequest for charitable and educational purposes in Preston amounted to £300,768, that is: for the erection of the Harris Free Public Library and Museum, £79,609; for forming the reference library and purchasing objects of art for the museum, £22,947; for an endowment fund £18,877; for the Harris Orphanage, £100,000; for the Harris Institute and technical education, £70,000; for the churches and schools, £6,335; for scholarships at the grammar school, £3,000.

Edmund Robert Harris had for a long time taken an interest in the public library movement in Preston. As we saw earlier, he was one of the members of the general committee for establishing a free library in 1854. Charles Roger Jacson noted that Edmund Robert Harris had left behind him in the provisions of his will the best possible evidences of his regard for the study and diffusion of taste and the cultivation of the humanising influences of society.

The provisions of his will give some indication as to the wealth which he possessed at his death. As well as Whinfield, he had property, buildings and stables and real estate in Preston, including some cottages in Gilbert Street; also land at Wrea near Hornby, houses and cottage in Ashton-upon-Ribble; stables in Preston—he bequeathed £10 to his groom Edward Bonney at the Preston stables; he had cottages at Kirkdale and at Croston also, and these were bequeathed to Joseph Cumming. He even owned the Rose and Crown in Much

Hoole which he bequeathed to Edward Bradley, his late clerk. The residue of his personal estate was to go to the governors of Queen Anne's Bounty fund for poor clergy.

Edmund Robert Harris was seventy-three when he died. He was unpretentious to the last for he wished that the institutions established using his money would be in remembrance of his father and his family, not of himself—although inevitably, as he possessed the same name, future generations would be bound to think of the benefactor possibly more than of his family. Within six months of his death, it was clear that there were moves afoot to link his name with the establishment of a permanent, purpose-built library and museum in Preston. The trustees of his will were Charles Roger Jacson of Barton Hall, John William Eccles, Revd Charles Harrison Wood of St George's Church, and David Irvin of Dilworth.

NOTES

1. 'Funeral sermon on the late E. R. Harris, Esq.,' *Preston Guardian*, 6 June 1877, p. 6.
2. Will of Edmund Robert Harris, Esq. of Whinfield, Ashton-upon-Ribble, 1877.

3

'A WORK OF PERMANENT VALUE AND AN EXAMPLE OF MEMORIAL ART' IS BORN

A T A MEETING on 1 May 1879, two important decisions were made by the council: firstly to acquire property on the east side of the market place, a plan for which was submitted to the council, showing that two new streets would be formed and that the future free public library and museum would occupy the site encompassed by two new streets, the market place and Lancaster Road; and secondly to approve a report for the foundation of a free public library and museum in association with the trustees of the late Edmund Robert Harris. The report, dated 12 February 1879, and signed by William Gilbertson and James Hibbert, indicated that the sub-committee previously set up to look into the establishment of the library had done its homework by visiting libraries already established in other towns, and was recommending a scheme for a permanent foundation of a library and museum, comprising sufficient accommodation to allow for future needs. The report suggested that the building should be noble in character and required a site which should be accessible, central and attractive; a site on the north or east side of the market place would exhibit the building to its best advantage—their preference was the east side, where it had 'complete severance of alignment from the Town Hall' thus avoiding a visual effect from the two buildings that might be 'mutually injurious'. The site, part of which had already been acquired, would comprise about 3,800 square yards, and cost about £25,000. They estimated that about £50,000 would be required for the building from the Harris trustees. It would house the Dr Shepherd Library, among other collections, and it was also suggested that money be allowed for books for the reference library, for museum objects, and an amount put in trust for the reference library, museum and art galleries. For their part, the corporation would provide books, periodicals, and newspapers for the lending library and newsroom, and would provide for the care and maintenance of the building 'in perpetuity'.[1] In October the trustees agreed to the idea, subject to the approval of the High Court of Justice (Chancery Division)—the letter was signed by Charles Roger Jacson, one of the four trustees; in it they suggested that the Avenham Institute be used for the art gallery and museum, rather than its being part of the free library; this idea does not seem to have been mentioned again. The corporation agreed to go ahead with the scheme as outlined in the report and to apply to parliament to obtain the rest of the site. The trustees agreed to a grant not exceeding £70,000 for the erection and maintenance of a free library in Preston; once the corporation had acquired the site, the trustees would submit a scheme for approval by the court. No mention seems to have been made up to this time of the design of the building.

The corporation made immediate steps to acquire the site for the building, and informed the public through the local papers of the move towards asking parliament for the powers to acquire the site for, and the erection of, a free library and museum, in conjunction with the trustees of E. R. Harris; a petition was duly submitted to the House of Commons. The outcome of the corporation's request to parliament was the Preston Improvement Act, 1880, which received the royal assent on 2 August 1880. Part of the title states it to be 'An Act to extend the Borough of Preston and to enable the Mayor, Aldermen, and Burgesses thereof to provide a Site for a Public Library and Museum'. Part of the Act granted the power to erect a free library using £70,000 of the estate of the late Edmund Robert Harris, and for the corporation to acquire a site at the estimated cost of £30,000. As regards the site, the Act enabled the corporation to make two new streets from the market place to Lancaster Road on the north and south sides of the proposed library and museum site, and to widen some surrounding roads; these works should be completed within fifteen years. The corporation could borrow money if required; expenses incurred in maintaining the public library and museum had to come from the borough fund; the rate limit for the public library and museum was 1½d in the pound.

The next three years saw the gradual transfer of ownership of property on the site to the corporation, the demolition of property and the extinction for ever of buildings, courts and streets very familiar to the inhabitants of Preston at the time. Pictures and photographs exist of the site prior to its clearance; one of the facade of buildings facing the market place; one of the public house called the Swan With Two Necks, and one showing the regulars outside the Blue Anchor Inn, which must have been one of the last buildings demolished, as the photograph is taken from the north and shows rubble underfoot. Into history passed Gin Bow Entry, Wilcockson's Court, the Strait (that is, narrow) Shambles (often mistakenly spelt 'Straight'), and Blue Anchor Court. The regulars at the Swan With Two Necks and other public houses would have to change their allegiance to other pubs, or perhaps spend their time improving themselves in the library! By August 1883, the corporation had spent £26,320 in purchasing and pulling down property on the site.

At its meeting of 28 April 1881, the corporation approved a draft scheme for the erection and endowment of the Harris Free Public Library and Museum. This was the first time that the design of the building became public; there seems to have been no competition for the design, for there is no evidence that any other designs than that submitted by James Hibbert, alderman and local architect, were considered. The building was to be of the Greek Ionic Order; James Hibbert wrote: 'Monumental art of Greece and Rome speaks a language the subtlest excellencies of which can reach and be appreciated by thousands of every race and clime. As long as civilisation lasts these excellencies will continue to speak an unvarying and imperishable language to unborn millions. Truly, they are eternal!'[2]

James Hibbert was born in Preston, son of Joseph and Hannah, and christened at St John's Church on 15 February 1833; his father was a sizer. He was educated at Preston Grammar School, and trained as an architect. He left Preston in 1851, and after time in Paris and Manchester, returned to his native town in 1855, mainly because of the illness of his elder sister Margaret Anne, who died later in that year. Professionally he went into partnership with Nathan Rainford, and in 1857 designed his first important building, the Baptist chapel in

James Hibbert, architect of the Harris. This was the last and most important building he designed in his career, described as 'one of the finest provincial Athenaeums in Europe.

Fishergate which still stands today. It was designed mainly in the Italian Romanesque style, but with the side windows of the Gothic Revival; Hibbert's opinion about architecture was that it depended 'not on style, but upon the individuality of the artist'; he was to be very versatile in the styles he adopted. His next two buildings were Italianate—the Mill Hill Congregational Chapel and the savings bank in Blackburn; the latter was completed in 1863, using the monumental Italian Palazzo style. He was also successful here in placing windows between columns, something he achieved with effect in the Harris building years later. In 1866 he designed the first of three churches in the Gothic Revival style, St Saviour's Church, Leeming Street; the others were St Matthew's (1880) and St James' in Avenham Lane (1881). In St James' Church, a stained glass window was designed and donated by Richard Newsham for the east transept, this being considered the most important of the eight windows he donated to various churches in Lancashire; Newsham also erected the upper decorated part of the tower as a memorial to his wife. James Hibbert married in 1865. He was a member of the Preston town council from 1871, and an alderman from 1874, and was mayor for the year 1880–81. As a member of the free library committee he was commissioned to report on the establishment of a permanent library and museum, and as a result travelled widely at home and abroad as part of this assignment. Soon after submitting the report, he was appointed architect of the building, and the Harris Free Public Library and Museum was the last and most important building of his career and described at the time as 'one of the finest provincial Athenaeums in Europe'. Once the building was open and in use, he resigned from the free library committee in 1895, and as alderman in March 1898; the council reported its desire 'to place on record its appreciation of the ability displayed, and the interest taken at all times by Mr Hibbert in the affairs of the Corporation during the many years he has been connected with the Council'.3 He then went to live in London, and died in Croydon towards the end of 1903 at the age of seventy.

A special committee was set up to oversee the erection and fitting up of the Harris Free Public Library and Museum, consisting of the Harris trustees and four members of the corporation. An Order in the High Court of Justice (Chancery Division) of the 24 July 1882 approved the 'Scheme for the Erection of the Free Public Library and Museum'. As part of this scheme the Harris trustees were to give the sum of £70,000 for the erection, furnishing and fitting of the building; also on or before the completion of the building, they were to give £15,000 for purchasing books for the reference library and objects and specimens for the museum, particularly those which would illustrate and promote the knowledge of the geology and natural history of Preston and its neighbourhood, and the 'industrial arts' and 'sciences' connected with it, and for obtaining specimens and examples of fine arts. On completion of the building and handing over to the corporation, the trustees would grant a further £15,000 as an endowment fund for the library and museum; the capital of this fund would be transferred to twelve trustees, called the endowment trustees, who would invest the sum. The income from the endowment fund would be used for providing additions to the reference library and museum. Thus at this stage the trustees were agreeing to spend a total of £100,000 on the scheme.[4]

By August 1882 the corporation had approved the plans submitted by the trustees and prepared by James Hibbert. These were accompanied by a report from the architect giving details of the proposed design. The building was to be classical in design and of the Ionic Order, with its chief features being 'simplicity and symmetry of plan, truthfulness of expression and refinement of detail'; this design was thought most suitable for a library and museum, being a repository of knowledge. The foundations were to be of rubble stone, and the outside walls would be faced with stone, backed with brickwork, the internal walls being of rubble stone and brickwork. Rising mains and hydrants would be provided on each floor for extinguishing fire, and the whole building would be warmed by either hot water or warm fresh air, and supplemented by open fireplaces if necessary. Ventilation would be provided by ducts to each department; fresh air would be drawn in from below and impure air carried away through ventilators located on the roof. On the ground and 'principal' (that is, first) floors, light would be provided by wide, lofty and numerous windows. On the second floor, the museum galleries, the central hall and staircase would be lighted from above. There should be sufficient entrances to the building for convenient and direct access to each department, and there should be a covered area for taking up and setting down for carriages and cabs in wet weather. The staircases should be double to regulate the up and down stream of visitors when the rooms are crowded. 'To secure quietude and freedom from interruption for the more studious class of readers, the Lending Department together with the Reading Room and Newsroom should not be on the same floor as the Reference Libraries.'

The collection of models and examples of industrial arts should be on the ground floor in the central hall and separate from the general museum collection of fine arts, the natural sciences and antiquities. The reference libraries as a distinct department of the foundation should occupy the whole of the principal floor. In the reference libraries, tables would be placed next to the large windows for light, and there would be accommodation for two hundred people. The museum galleries should occupy the whole of the upper (that is, second) floor, one side devoted to the fine arts, including a permanent collection which would be built up over time, and exhibitions; another to natural history and physics—it would be partly furnished by the collection in the museum at Cross Street, with purchases from the South Kensington Museum; the remaining side to general archaeology, ceramic and finer kinds of industrial art, and illustrations of ethnology. The horizontal division into three storeys was considered to give external dignity and importance to the building which was needed if it was not to be dominated by the neo-Gothic town hall. In the reading room and news room attached to the lending department there would be accommodation for 276 people. The plans allowed for expansion to 30,350 volumes in the lending library—at that time there were about 10,000 volumes; 5,000 volumes in the Library of Patents on the ground floor—the number stood at that time at 3,400 volumes; the Harris (reference) library allowed expansion to 40,289 volumes— there was none at the time, but the £15,000 provided in the scheme would purchase 20,000 volumes for the Harris reference library to begin with; and for the Dr Shepherd Library, at that time containing 8,300 volumes, room was provided for over 14,000 volumes.

The rooms were to be built of sufficient height for galleries to be built if necessary in the future, to be accessed from iron staircases, although at the time it was thought unlikely that they would be required 'within any measurable distance of time'; in recent years mezzanine floors have been constructed in the north and east galleries of the first floor, and in the east gallery of the second floor. In the 1980s, plans were drawn up for mezzanine floors in the reference library also, only to be turned down by English Heritage as not suitable in this Grade 1 listed building. The central hall and staircase would be used mainly for sculpture of both the antique and later schools. Friezes and metopes of the Parthenon, the Temple of Theseus at Athens and the Temple of Apollo Epicurius at Phigaleia in Arcadia could be arranged to form a permanent architectonic decoration of these parts of the interior.

'There are fashions in architecture, as in most artistic productions of the time. A structure that is fit for its uses subserves its distinctive functions, and is in harmony of expression with the nature and quality of those functions, stands above the fluctuations of ephemeral taste. Such, in this instance, is the object to be sought and endeavoured; so far as the Building is concerned—the production of a work of permanent value, and example of memorial art'.[5]

The suggestion for the ceremonial laying of the foundation stone for the new building was first mooted in June 1881, when it was hoped that the Prince of Wales might be able to perform the ceremony during the Guild Merchant of the following year. The Guild committee made the request to the Prince of

Lord Derby speaking at the laying of the foundation stone of the Harris building, 5 September 1882;
the foundation stone was laid by the Earl of Lathom.
(Supplement to the *Illustrated London News*, 16 Sept 1882.)

Wales in May 1892, but he had to decline, as he did not expect to be in the country during the Guild week in September. In July it was decided to ask the Duke and Duchess of Albany instead, and they accepted the invitation; but at the last minute they too were unable to come owing to the duke's illness. By this time thousands of medals had been struck commemorating the laying of the foundation stone by the Duke of Albany, and twenty thousand programmes had been printed, which turned out to be worthless; further medals were struck in a great hurry showing the Earl of Lathom instead; he performed the ceremony in the presence of the Duke of Cambridge. The Earl of Lathom was chosen because of his position as deputy grand master of the freemasons, as the council had resolved that the 'Foundation Stone of the Harris Free Public Library and Museum should be laid with Masonic Ceremonial'.

The weather was not good on Tuesday 5 September 1882; there was a steady and persistent drizzle. But at least the main participants in this important occasion would have the benefit of cover from a large marquee erected over the site for the building. After a masonic procession around the streets of central Preston, and the procession of the Duke of Cambridge from the guild hall, attended by the mayor and corporation, the Harris trustees and others, the foundation stone was laid sometime after 1.00 p.m. by the Earl of Lathom, who had received a trumpet fanfare as he entered the marquee. At the ceremony the Earl of Lathom was presented with a trowel as a memento of the occasion by Charles Roger Jacson on behalf of the Harris trustees. The ceremonial trowel was made by Elkington and Co. at a cost of £41 13s. od. A person looking for the foundation stone today will seek in vain. A drawing at the time suggests that it would be at basement level of the building; the *Preston Herald* describes it as being laid in the 'north-western corner of the site' (that is, the corner of the market place and Harris Street); some believe that it is in the central part of the building which is totally sealed—perhaps it requires a latter-day Howard Carter to unravel the mystery! Coins and an inscribed copper plate were placed on a lower stone, and the foundation stone was laid on top, thus sealing the plate and coins; there was no wording on the stone itself, but the inscription on the plate read out to the assembled throng was

THIS FOUNDATION STONE

OF A

FREE PUBLIC LIBRARY AND MUSEUM

TO BE ERECTED BY MEANS OF FUNDS PROVIDED BY THE TRUSTEES

OF THE WILL OF

EDMUND ROBERT HARRIS

OF THIS TOWN

ON A SITE GIVEN BY THE CORPORATION

OF

THE BOROUGH OF PRESTON

WAS LAID BY

THE RIGHT HONOURABLE THE EARL OF LATHOM

D.G.M. IN FREEMASONRY OF THE GRAND LODGE OF

ENGLAND, AND PROV. G.M. OF WEST LANCASHIRE

ON TUESDAY, SEPTEMBER 5TH, 1882

DURING THE CELEBRATION OF THE GUILD MERCHANT

IN THE 46TH YEAR OF THE REIGN OF

HER MOST GRACIOUS MAJESTY QUEEN VICTORIA

On 5 October 1882 the committee set up to oversee the building of the Harris approved the report and the plans by James Hibbert. The final approval of the plans by the corporation was given on 29 March 1883 and by May these plans had been approved by the judge in the High Court. So the scene was now set for the growth of this great scheme.

NOTES

1. 'Report to the Free Library Committee of a scheme for the foundation of a public library and museum in association with the Harris Trustees' in J. Hibbert (ed.), *Notes on Free Public Libraries and Museums* (Preston, 1881).
2. *Ibid.*, p. 103.
3. Preston Borough Council Minutes, 1897–8, meeting of 31 March 1898, pp. 112–4.
4. Scheme for the Erection of a Free Public Library and Museum by the Harris Trustees, at Preston, Lancashire. In the High Court of Justice, Chancery Division, July 1882.
5. Hibbert, James, 'A Report to accompany the design for the Harris Free Public Library and Museum', July 1882.

4

THE SCHEME GROWS TO FRUITION

THE BUILDING COMMITTEE wasted no time in advertising for tenders for the erection of the building, both in local papers, such as the *Preston Guardian*, the *Preston Herald* and the *Preston Chronicle*, and in other regional and national publications. The work was divided into four sections, the first one of which included the majority of the work to be done: 1. Excavator and drainer, mason, waller, bricklayer and paviour, fireproof flooring and roofing, ironfounder, warming and ventilating; 2. Carpenter and joiner; 3. Plasterer; 4. Plumber, glazier and painter. The tenders had to be received by Saturday 1 September 1883. When the tenders were opened on 3 September, there had been several tenders received for each section. On 1 October it was resolved to accept the tender of the Preston firm Cooper & Tullis for sections 1 and 3, and the decision on the other two sections was deferred.

On 25 October, the council resolved that 'the site (2745 superficial square yards) be appropriated for the Harris Free Public Library and Museum' and the following day the chairman of the building committee reported that he had received two more tenders—these must have been received after the closing date for tenders—from Mr Walmsley, for sections 2 and 4; it was agreed that these be put in with the rest; eventually it was this John Walmsley who got the contract for sections 2 and 4. Meanwhile it was agreed that the architect, James Hibbert, be paid 5 per cent of the cost of the building, provided that the building costs were no higher than £62,000.

Work began on the building in October 1883, more than a year after the foundation stone had been laid; the hoarding round the site was in place by the 20th; early excavations found some interesting coins, including a Manchester promissory halfpenny of 1783. In the course of building over the next few years the original plans were slightly modified: in March 1884 James Hibbert's plan for an extended basement under the news room and reading room was adopted at an extra cost of £200. At a meeting of the building committee on 7 February 1887 the architect recommended that the height of the lantern be raised by three courses of plain stone at an extra cost of £200; this was agreed. Later in the year

The pedimental sculpture 'The Age of Pericles' carved by Edwin Roscoe Mullins
The figures on the pediment from left to right represent: Thucydides meditating on unwritten history;
Socrates, Zeno and Parmenides, philosophers; the Victor of the Games; Ictinus, chief architect of the
Parthenon; Anaxagoras; Pericles, commander and statesman; Pindar, poet; Pheidias, the great
sculptor, with shield; chariot horses; Aeschylus meditating upon Athens' future; Sophocles and Euripides
conversing upon foreign arts; and Herodotus, the historian.

it was agreed that the building be wired for electric light and the contract went to Strode & Co. at a cost of £790.

By March 1885 it first became apparent that the cost of the building was going to exceed the figure of £70,000 quoted in the original scheme; a further sum of £5,000 was sanctioned by the court on 18 May for the completion of the building, including a group of sculptures for the pediment on the front of the building. After a discussion on the pedimental sculpture, the committee authorised James Hibbert to plan the sculptures and investigate possible sculptors; the total cost was not to exceed £3,000. Nearly a year was to pass before it was finally decided in May 1886 to accept a contract worth £2,700 with Mr Edwin Roscoe Mullins, after seeing a model of the sculpture, the work to be completed within two years.

Edwin Roscoe Mullins was born in London in 1848, and after a time in Munich, he returned to London in 1874 and became a constant exhibitor at the Royal Academy and other galleries. As well as individual works such as a bronze statue of 'Boy with a Top' exhibited at the Royal Academy in 1895, he executed works on many buildings in London, as well as the pedimental sculpture entitled 'The Age of Pericles' for the Harris Free Public Library and Museum. He also produced a frieze representing the entry of Charles II into London for the drawing room of the Grocers Hall in 1892. He died in Suffolk in 1907.

By the end of 1886, three of the figures for the pedimental sculpture had been received in Preston from Roscoe Mullins in London; they were stored in the 'stone yard', in the absence of any better accommodation; the other sculptures followed in stages. Later, in 1888, questions were raised about the pedimental sculpture which by this time was in place. The committee were of the opinion that 'there is a want of sufficient accentuation of the drapery of the figures throughout; that some of the figures at each end of the pediment especially Thucydides, Socrates, Zeno and Herodotus are placed too far back with reference to the Corona of the Cornice and that there is too great a gap between Parmenides and the Runner'.[1] It seems as though their comments were not heeded, as neither the architect nor the sculptor agreed with them; the committee were forced to back down as they concluded that they were precluded by the terms of the agreement from interfering between the sculptor and the architect. In a letter to the sculptor, the building committee expressed the view that the 'sculpture deserves to be specially admired for the boldness and characteristic expression of the figures and the dramatic interest of the composition'; it was considered second only to those at the British Museum and St George's Hall, Liverpool.

Building work progressed from the end of 1883 until 1889, with occasional delays for bad weather and the difficulty of obtaining the correct type of stone. In May 1884 there were twenty masons working on the site, and five wallers. The contractors were hoping that the central hall would be covered in by the end of 1886, towards the end of which year visitors to the market place would have seen the columns at the facade of the building rising—forty-two stones were required in total for the six columns so familiar today; by this time ten of these stones had been put in place as well as almost all the thirty-six iron girders required for the shell of the building. In February 1888 the contractors Cooper and Tullis were estimating that the plastering of the building would be completed by September of that year and in January of the following year copies of the Parthenon, Phigaleian and Appyrian friezes were ordered to be purchased from the British Museum. By this time the ironmongery used in the building was put in place—Charles Smith supplied the iron work within the building; the huge iron gates at the entrances, the internal staircase and railings were supplied by the Coalbrookdale Co. Ltd.

At the beginning of 1890 a watchman, William Worthington, had been appointed at £1 per week; and the first cleaner, John Jackson, began work in July 1890, earning just £1 per week. The building was being heated by 1890, as bills were paid for coke from the Preston Gas Company.

The good progress that had been maintained from 1883 onwards evaporated in 1889 amid legal wrangles, and it was to be another four years before the building was ready for its official opening. It was clearly almost completed in 1889, for the building committee in October of that year were asking that they be informed when the building would be ready to receive books, as they had the £15,000 set aside for purchasing books; there is no evidence that the information was given at this time. The trustees' solicitor informed the committee in March 1890 that there seemed to be insufficient money to complete the building. A special meeting was called to resolve the problem, which was still not solved by August when the contractors Cooper & Tullis completed their work; John Walmsley completed his contract in the following month. There were still outstanding claims for money from both contractors, and also from James Hibbert. There was much discussion between the parties. It was to be June 1892 before agreement was reached between the architect and the building committee, after the trustees had agreed to use their suspense account which had been set aside for unforeseen contingencies; James Hibbert brought to the meeting of that month the designs, drawings and estimates for the completion of the building—these included plans for the pavings, designs for gas standard lamps and designs for twenty-eight pendants for gas and electric light. The architect was also authorised to obtain from Messrs Bell & Coupland model bookcases, tables and chairs for the reference library for consideration and approval. Drawings of walnut bookcases nine feet high in three divisions were considered a week later. A model bookcase, table and chair were considered in August; the prices would be £45 for each bookcase, £13 per table and £3 per chair. Meanwhile the free public library committee had obtained a grant of £500 from the Department of Science and Art towards the purchase of certain reproductions in plaster; the selection made by the chairman of the committee, James Hibbert, included *David, Guiliano de' Medici,* and *Lorenzo de' Medici* by Michelangelo, various Greek and Roman examples, and the eastern pediment of the Parthenon. Initially the committee thought this purchase unwise because of the financial problems they were experiencing, but the purchases were authorised in December.

In March 1893, Joseph V. Hibbert was engaged as architect for the furnishing and fitting of the lending library and other rooms; John Heywood of Manchester was contracted to fit and furnish the lending library and patents library. For readers' tables, chairs and newspaper stands, Gillow & Co. of Lancaster were given the contract.

By July it had been agreed between the council and the building committee that delivery of the building should take place soon, and discussion took place about the ceremonial opening. The penultimate meeting of the building committee took place on 18 August 1893, in the room which was to become the

Reproduction of the tomb of Lorenzo de' Medici by Michelangelo, with attendant.

reference library. The trustees transferred the following amounts to the corporation

£ 454 16s. 11d. from Science and Art Department etc.
£ 300 0s. 0d. museum benches and cases
£5402 4s. 8d. cash balance of books etc., fund account
£8346 15s. 0d. Midland Railway 4 per cent perpetual preference stock
£1328 5s. 0d. 4 per cent perpetual guaranteed preferential stock
£1483 0s. 0d. London, Brighton and South Coast Railway
                     preferential 5 per cent stock.

On receiving an acknowledgement that the mayor and corporation were satisfied, the trustees and building committee would immediately hand over the keys and possession of the building and premises to the corporation. Before separating, the committee recorded their appreciation of the invaluable services of the chairman, Charles Roger Jacson, and of the tact, wisdom, courtesy and good sense with which he had presided over the proceedings. In the speeches prior to actually handing over the keys, Charles Roger Jacson, for the building committee, congratulated the mayor on the acquisition of so valuable a property and an institution that was calculated to do such a great amount of good for the community, and hoped the work done by the building committee was satisfactory. In reply, the mayor, Thomas Edelston, expressed satisfaction at the work, every step of which had been done with the best intentions and the utmost integrity. He thanked the committee on behalf of the townspeople for their arduous and responsible task. He himself was grateful to be the one to receive the new building, as thirty-five years previously he had been involved in the movement for establishing a free public library. Also they remembered Edmund Robert Harris and the trustees and the money donated for various causes for the benefit of the townspeople. He was very happy to take possession of the building, 'and I hope it will fully answer the purpose for which it is intended, and afford intellectual entertainment and improvement for generations unborn of the people of Preston and the surrounding neighbourhood'. After further speeches, Charles Roger Jacson handed the keys to the mayor. The hope was that the public would soon be in the new building, and out of the 'crowded, stuffy place in the Town Hall'.

Within a few weeks, Charles Roger Jacson, who had contributed so much to public service in the town, and particularly to bringing to fruition the Harris Free Public Library and Museum Scheme, had died. The council recorded that for a long time he had been

> an honoured and most valuable Member of this Corporation, when by his high intellect, great abilities and charm of manner rendered conspicuous and invaluable Service to the Community at large, and endeared his Memory for all time. It is with the deepest regret that on the occasion of the culmination of one of his most signal Works, the Opening Ceremonial of the Harris Free Public Library and Museum, to the success of which so much is due to the ability displayed by him as one of the Trustees of the Harris Trust Funds—his presence will be wanting, thereby depriving the Ceremonial of one of its brightest Ornaments . . .[2]

A marble memorial tablet to Charles Roger Jacson was unveiled by the Earl of Derby in June 1895, in the east room on the second floor—it is now to be seen on the staircase between the first and second floors; the memorial was placed in recognition of 'his manifold public services and high character'.

NOTES

1. Minute Book of the Harris Trustees, 1882–9, meeting of Monday 3 September 1888.
2. Preston Borough Council Minutes, 1892–3, p. 308.

5

Achiev'd is the Glorious Work!

THURSDAY 26 OCTOBER 1893 was indeed a day for popular rejoicing, for the Harris building was at last to be officially opened, even if it would be several more weeks before people would be using it for its rightful purpose. The Earl and Countess of Derby and the Earl and Countess of Lathom were met by the mayor, Alderman Edelston, at Preston railway station, and waving and cheering crowds lined the route as their carriages made their way to the town hall along Fishergate; the procession included members of the free library committee and the Harris trustees. As the procession reached the town hall, where the crowd was even bigger, the band of the 2nd Battalion East Yorkshire Regiment struck up with *Stanley for Ever*; the guests alighted at the town hall, and then proceeded to the guild hall for the reception of all the guests by the mayor and Miss Edelston. The guild hall had been specially decorated with ferns, firs and palms covering the whole of the platform, and special carpeting laid down, with easy chairs, ottomans, divans and sofas arranged around the room; the mayor in his robes and chain of office then received the guests in this colourful and balmy environment. Bouquets of flowers were presented to the Countess of Lathom and to Lady Derby by a group of young children.

As the clock on the town hall struck one, the long procession began to make its way from the guild hall along Cheapside and on reaching the marketplace the participants could join the throng of people admiring the massive monument with its classical Athenian form and detail seen to its best advantage on one of the highest points of central Preston; the main entrance was in view with its wide flight of steps and six columns of the Ionic Order topped by the pedimental sculpture of heroic size showing some of the great names from the Age of Pericles, and above it the lamp of learning together with the dedication on the entablature reminding everyone of the purpose of the building

TO LITERATURE ARTS AND SCIENCES

The more ambitious would then try to recall the Greek learned in their school days, and begin translating the sentence from Pericles' funeral oration by Thucydides—as this surrounds all four sides of the frieze of the central lantern atop the building they would have to wait till later to read the whole inscription which, translated, reads

> For the whole earth is the sepulchre of illustrious men; not only are they commemorated by columns and inscriptions intheir own country, but in foreign lands there dwells also an unwritten memorial of them, graven, not upon stone, but in the hearts of men.

These illustrious men are alluded to again in the inscription at the foot of the central sculptures of the pediment; taken from Byron's *Manfred*, it reads

> The dead but sceptred Sovrans, who still rule
> Our spirits from their urns . . .

On reaching the east side of the market place the procession divided into two, with one group entering the Harris building through the gates in Jacson Street, and the other through the gates in Harris Street. The former group, before sweeping in through the gateway would ponder on the entablature's declaration

> ON EARTH THERE IS NOTHING GREAT BUT MAN;
> IN MAN THERE IS NOTHING GREAT BUT MIND

while the latter group would no doubt be encouraged by the promise

> THE MENTAL RICHES YOU MAY HERE ACQUIRE
> ABIDE WITH YOU ALWAYS

(The precept: 'REVERENCE IN MAN THAT WHICH IS SUPREME' can be seen on the remaining side of the building).

The guests mounted the steps and great cheers from the assembled crowd greeted their appearance at the portico; 'at this point the scene was a most impressive one. The magnificent building which was to be opened in a few moments stood out in bold view across the large square, now filled by a multitude which cheered with enthusiasm as the steps of the building became covered with the well known figures of prominent townsmen, with the noble guests in their midst.'[1] The band, positioned in front of the building, played a variety of airs now and during the remainder of the ceremony, such as the overture to *Mirella*, by Gounod, and *Haddon Hall* by Sullivan.

Once all the guests had assembled on the steps, the mayor presented Lord Derby with the key specially designed for the occasion. The key, designed and made by Alfred Gilbert, showed the arms of Preston and those of Lord Derby, together with a symbol of learning in the form of a pure rock crystal, around which ornamentation containing the three letters H (for Harris), and PP was arranged; it was made of iron and silver. The key is held permanently in the Victoria and Albert Museum; it is being loaned to the Harris Museum for the centenary celebrations of 1993. Lord Derby accepted the key, and without more ado unlocked the door to the Harris Free Public Library and Museum and entered, followed by the party of guests. The party then proceeded to the central hall where a dais, with palms and shrubs in the background, had been erected for the main guests. Those who could not find room on this floor looked on from the galleries above. Now followed about an hour of speeches; and the proceedings were opened with a prayer in which the Venerable Archdeacon Hornby asked that

> Almighty God be pleased to prosper this Institution which today is opened . . . grant that this Free Library may be the means of spreading abroad that knowledge which is profitable for man . . . Grant that those who manage the affairs of this 'Free Library' may be guided in all they do by the spirit of a sound mind, and may all who seek instruction here find that knowledge which may add to their happiness in this world, and make them wise unto salvation through Our Lord Jesus Christ, in whose name we offer up this prayer—Amen.[2]

The Bijou Naval Orchestra, with a chorus of about thirty voices, played and sang a selection from Haydn's *Creation*, which included the chorus

> Achiev'd is the glorious work;
> The Lord beholds it, and is pleased
> In lofty strains let us rejoice
> Our song let be the praise of God.

The mayor then called on Lord Derby to declare the building open. Lord Derby paid tribute to the late Charles Roger Jacson, and also to Alderman Hibbert; and then said 'I venture to congratulate you, Mr Mayor, as the representative of your fellow citizens, upon the great acquisition your town has made, and in the name of those who have called upon me to fulfil the duty, I beg to declare the Harris Free Public Library open for the benefit and the blessing of Mr Harris's fellow-townsmen'.[3]

Alderman Hibbert, as chairman of the free library committee, gave a vote of thanks to Lord Derby, and concluding said 'we Prestonians . . . have founded this Corporate institution, visible in a princely monument to the Harris name, where literature, the arts, and sciences may be enshrined, forming a real and true university of instruction for our youth, a recreation in the high sense of the word for our men and women, and a source of wealth of that kind which we have been bold to inscribe—will abide with them—always.'⁴

Lord and Lady Derby and the other principal guests were then conducted over the building, during which time the Bijou Naval Orchestra played the introductory march from *The Coronation* by Ellenberg. At the close of proceedings, the National Anthem was played, and the party returned to the town hall. A mayoral banquet took place at 3.00 p.m. in the public hall, which had been specially decorated and furnished.

Lord Derby, who declared the Harris building open on 26 October 1893, 'for the benefit of and the blessing of Mr Harris's fellow-townsmen.'

The final event of this momentous day in the history of the town was a 'conversazione' held in the Harris building in the evening at which over two thousand guests thronged the 'brilliantly lighted halls and galleries'. At 7.00 p.m., Lord and Lady Derby were being entertained at the Bull Hotel by the mayor, and it was 8.30 p.m. before this party proceeded to the Harris building and received the guests at the dais in the central hall on the ground floor. A little later the party moved into the south reading room, which had been extemporised as a concert hall; an excellent concert was given by Mr Joseph Cantor's Quartette Party, the chief vocalist being Madame Laura Smart; songs included *It was a dream*, *Bid me discourse*, and *L'Ardita*; and Mr Ben Roberts' rendering of *The Anchor's Weighed* was a great success.

Lord and Lady Derby and principal guests left the concert to have a tour of the building under the 'ciceronage'—what a wonderful word!—of the Revd Jonathan Shortt; the tour paid special reference to the Assyrian and Greek friezes. The guests would have mounted the stairs to the dizzy heights of the top gallery to view the Assyrian frieze showing events from the life of Ashur-

Nasir-Pal II who ruled the Assyrian Empire from 883 to 859 BC. The reliefs show the king at war besieging strongly walled towns, hunting wild bulls and lions and many other scenes; this 'sculpture reached an excellence unknown before. Bas-reliefs especially of the king and man-headed or eagle-headed beings performing acts of worship exhibit simplicity of design and reverence and dignity'.[5] Descending to the second floor, the guests would have been shown a copy of the frieze from the east side of the Parthenon showing the procession which took place at the festival celebrated every four years in Athens in honour of Athene; above the frieze are metopes from the south side of the Parthenon, showing combat between Lapiths and Centaurs. Descending to the first floor, the guests would have enjoyed viewing a more compact frieze showing the battles between Greeks and Amazons, this being a copy of the frieze discovered in the Temple of Apollo Epicurios, near the ancient Phigaleia in Arcadia. All these friezes are still in the building today—one frieze which the guests would not have seen is the Alexander frieze on the ground floor, which was presented to the museum and art gallery in 1987: it portrays the triumphal entry of Alexander the Great into the city of Babylon; this cast was taken from a marble version of the frieze made by Bertel Thorvaldsen (1770–1843).

The *Preston Guardian* reported that the

> view of the interior from the high galleries was enchanting in the extreme. Everybody was struck with the beautiful harmony in the proportions of the building. The introduction of light and life in the brilliant illumina-tions and the gay crown completed a picture which will not be soon forgotten by those who saw it. Looking from the topmost gallery in the lantern—an almost dizzy height—one can take in at a glance almost the whole of the architectural features of the central hall, and here it is that the beautiful symmetry of the structure can be best observed. Down away on the ground floor, on the circular patch of variegated marbles, destined to receive shortly the colossal statue of David and other reproductions of Michelangelo's works, the Bijou Naval Orchestra are performing a selection of music, and the melodious strains float upwards, ravishing the ear at the same time that the eye is captivated by the brilliant and unique spectacle.[6]

There was an exhibition of scientific instruments in the picture gallery, which included Edison's phonograph—Lord Derby responded to a request to deliver a short address into the funnel; his voice was recorded on the prepared cylinder, which was voice-signed 'Derby' and presented to the museum. The National Electric Supply Company and Mr S. Heap exhibited electrical apparatus; the Electric Light Company showed examples of various electric meters; Mr Heap

'Looking from the topmost gallery in the lantern—an almost dizzy height—one can take in at a glance almost the whole architectural features of the central hall, and here it is that the beautiful symmetry of the structure can best be observed.'
(*Preston Guardian* reporting after the opening ceremony in October 1893; photograph taken in 1993.)

also exhibited various domestic electrical appliances, such as electric fans, irons and ovens. On top of the building, a brilliant searchlight gave a remarkable display, lighting up several distant parts of the town.

One of the most interesting and popular displays was in rooms set aside for a show of microscopic and other apparatus, organised by Councillors Dunn and Healey. About thirty instruments were lent by gentlemen in the town and Messrs Woolley of Manchester. The post office contributed a collection of telegraphic appliances, including a specimen of the Holyhead to Howth (Dublin) cable, and a piece of the first submarine cable ever laid (Dover to Calais), that had been under the water for twenty-five years.

Lord and Lady Derby left the gathering at about 10.00 p.m., in order to catch a train to Knowsley. The mayor said goodbye at the entrance to the building. At 10 o'clock the band moved to the upper rooms where the guests danced away the final hours of this momentous day.

Much work still needed to be done to transfer books from the town hall to the new building in time to open the building for public use on Monday 1

Originally the reading room had separate areas for men and women. This photograph, taken in the 1890s, is of the women's section with the men's seen in the distance. Attendants, standing on the left by the pillar, supervised the room.

January 1894; even so, only the lending library, the newsroom and reading room were opened to the public at this time. Not surprisingly, despite the freezing weather, there were more books issued on that day than on any day since the free library was opened fifteen years previously; there were also a great many visitors to see the new institution, although only the ground floor was open during the day. The mayor, John Holden, held an 'At Home' in the evening of the opening day, a reception taking place on a dais, backed by the corporation insignia and a mass of choice foliage on the first floor. It was estimated that over one-fifth of the population of the borough visited the building during the day, with five or six thousand present in the evening.

A design fault soon showed itself: the side doors were used for people to gain access to the newsroom from Jacson Street and to the reading room from Harris Street; the constant opening of these doors, accompanied by the wintry blasts, played havoc with the newspapers and made life uncomfortable and inconvenient for all; these doors were therefore closed and entry was gained from the central hall—this is still the case today. In the reading room, initially the tables nearest to the librarian's counter were set apart for ladies, but later the accommodation was divided equally, the ladies having the part of the room nearest Lancaster Road.

Although part of the building was now open for business, much work still needed to be done to get the other departments up and running. In February 1894 Messrs Joseph and Arnett Hibbert were requested to prepare and submit a scheme and estimate for setting up of the reproductions, and displaying them on suitable pedestals. Donations received included miniature casts of the friezes of the Parthenon from Mrs Jacson, and from the trustees of Edmund Robert Harris a portrait in oils of the Revd Robert Harris, by J. Barker. During this time the objects from the museum at Cross Street, and books in the Dr Shepherd and Patents Libraries, were transferred to the new building, as were the Newsham and Arundel collections—the latter collection of reproductions of paintings in frescoes were hung in the north gallery on the principal floor, which, if the original plans had been adhered to, would have housed the Harris reference library. The museum, and the picture and sculpture galleries were eventually opened to the public on 1 January 1896.

In June 1895 William Bramwell was appointed to form the Harris reference library; he was also at this time librarian of the Dr Shepherd Library, which had re-opened to the public in the Harris building on Monday 8 April 1895. Richard Shepherd is reputed to have been born near Kendal in 1694, and came to Preston to practise as a doctor. He was admitted as a Freeman of the Borough in 1724. He was elected alderman in 1746, and was mayor twice, in 1747–8, and in 1755–6; he died in 1761. In his will he bequeathed 'all and every my Books of what kind or Nature soever unto my Executors . . . in trust for the benefit of the Mayor and Aldermen of this Borough'; he gave money for fitting up and shelving an appropriate room for the library; and directed that no book 'shall be lent or removed out of such library but shall always remain to be there read'; there should be two keys for the room—one to be kept by the mayor, and the other by the librarian; he left endowments to pay a librarian, and also for buying

Dr Richard Shepherd, 1694–1761, who bequeathed his library to the Corporation of Preston; the Shepherd Library is now housed in the Harris building.

books.[7] The Harris building was the fourth home of the Dr Shepherd Library. The library was administered by its own board of management and since James Hibbert had been chairman, had increased significantly the number of books in it; no money was taken from the rates for the Dr Shepherd Library. New additions included books on literature, art, science, history, archaeology, and philosophy; it was rich in the publications of learned societies—Chetham, Camden, Surtees, Holbein and Dilettanti Societies, Record Society publications and local and county histories.

The Harris reference library itself seems to have opened at about the same time as the museum and art gallery, for the *Preston Herald* on 4 January 1896 quotes Councillor Hamilton at a council meeting as saying that several books had been added to the reference library 'and were placed for the use of the public in the room on the right hand side of the upper floor'.

Up to the end of the century there were some notable donations to the Harris including a marble bust of Miss Harris (Edmund Robert's sister) from the council of the Harris Institute; a present of a cast of the head of Lemnian Athena from Bologna, where the original is kept—the corporation returned the favour with an album of photographs of the Harris Free Public Library and Museum. A vestibule was constructed in the entrance hall. By now people were coming in from far and wide to use the library, museum and picture galleries.

NOTES

1. *Preston Guardian*, Saturday 28 October 1893, p. 9.
2. *Ibid.*, p. 9.
3. *Ibid.*, p. 10.
4. *Ibid.*, p. 10.
5. E. A. Wallis Budge (ed.), *Assyrian Sculptures in the British Museum* (British Museum, 1914).
6. *Preston Guardian*, Saturday 28 October 1893, p. 5.
6. Shepherd, Will of Richard, late of Preston, Esq., 1777.

6

THE LIBRARY IN THE TWENTIETH CENTURY

LENDING LIBRARY

THE LENDING LIBRARY today is very different from the one known to James Hibbert, William Bramwell and their contemporaries: the silent glide of light pen across bar-code, recording the loan of a book, is registered instantaneously on a mainframe computer in Lancashire County Library headquarters in Corporation Street; the catalogue of books in the library is on the same computer, and can be searched instantaneously too—gone are the days of the inflexible printed catalogues, expensive to produce, and even their successors the card indexes are virtually obsolete; as well as books, videos and compact discs, records and cassettes are loaned out; gone is the dark, heavy furniture, replaced by more appropriate and light bookcases and staff desks; there is much more colour, the whole brightly lit by adequate fluorescent lighting; readers' advisers, and a supermarket-type open access approach to the shelves that was unthinkable to those who founded the library. What would be familiar to them would be the constant bustle and thronging of people thirsting for knowledge and entertainment as on the day the library opened in 1894; in the year ending March 1993, over half a million visits were made to the lending and music libraries. The lending library occupies the east side of the ground floor, and continues round both sides of the building as far as the side doors on Jacson Street and Harris Street; the music library occupies the market square end of the south side, separated from the lending library by the library staff workroom. Of all the departments within the Harris building, the lending library is the most heavily patronised.

As the nineteenth century gave way to the twentieth, the lending library had become well established in the Harris building, and the amount of public interest in it was undiminished. In 1901 the number of issues was 112,567 and in the following year 125,894; the number spasmodically increased to 140,000 by 1912. Book selection was shared between the librarian and a sub-committee of the free library committee. The librarian, William Bramwell, retired in February 1916, having been in charge of the free library since August 1879; he was replaced in the following year by William Bright Barton, who had already been art director and curator since 1895; he was chief librarian until his retirement in 1925.

In 1919, the method of issuing books using the card-charging method was introduced, instead of the previous method of entering details in a ledger. It was at this time also that the system of classifying books which had been in use now for forty years, was being replaced, first in the reference library, followed in 1920 by the lending department. The new classification was the Dewey decimal classification, the main headings of which were (and to a great extent still are):

0   General Works
1   Philosophy
2   Religion
3   Social Sciences
4   Languages
5   Natural Science
6   Useful Arts
7   Fine Arts
8   Literature
9   History, Biography, Travels.

One result of the reclassification was an increase in the use of all the above classes, except fiction: between 1920 and 1930 issues nearly doubled. Indexes were provided—a subject catalogue on cards; an author catalogue, and an alphabetical subject index.

The lending library was closed from 25 August until 1 October 1923, in order that it be remodelled to allow for an open access system, where the public could browse and choose books for themselves on the shelves, instead of locating titles of books via the catalogues and then asking staff for them. This revolutionary change was very popular and attracted many new readers; by 1925 there were over fourteen thousand registered readers. In this same year the reserved book system was introduced, where readers could reserve books which were normally in stock but were currently out on loan; this service was much appreciated. Frank Helliwell, the assistant librarian, was appointed chief librarian from 1 April 1925.

Campaigning against cruelty to animals is not a modern phenomenon—in 1920 the library received a donation from the Anti-Vivisection Society entitled: *Great Testimony Against Scientific Cruelty*. In December 1922 the committee passed a resolution to 'expunge racing news' from the newspapers in the free library; a similar motion was passed again in June 1932, and this policy lasted until the early 1950s. Tentative moves towards using modern forms of communication and technology occurred in the 1920s when a telephone extension was provided to the

View of the busy lending library counter in 1935.
Book issues almost doubled in the early years of the 1930s.

librarian's desk, and a typewriter purchased for the incredible amount of £25. It would be 1946 before the first duplicator was purchased—for £45!

By the mid-twenties the lending section was feeling the pressure of increased usage to the extent that it was being suggested that 'distributing stations' should be set up in the outlying districts of the borough. The situation was relieved somewhat by issuing books to boys and girls through school libraries. It was first suggested by the Lancashire County Council that the county and the borough should co-operate in establishing a branch library or distributing centre at Ribbleton; later a suggestion was adopted that in the Ribbleton parish room there should be a small branch library established, as long as it could be used by both Preston and county ratepayers; this was opened in March 1927. In 1934 this became the sole responsibility of Preston Borough Council.

Frank Helliwell resigned his position as chief librarian in January 1928 to move to a similar post in the borough of Southwark. On the 12 September 1928, Joseph Pomfret of Darwen was appointed chief librarian.

Throughout the late 1920s the number of issues per year was slightly over 220,000; then, because of the chronic economic situation and depression, the numbers rose in the years 1930 to 1933 from 276,000 to 433,000 and by 1933 the number of borrowers had increased to 21,383, which was about 18 percent of the population.

A major change in the organisation of the library occurred in 1935 when the men's reading room and news room were transferred to the town hall, to allow the establishment of a children's library in the Harris building. The library remained open throughout the war, but was subject to black-out regulations. On 18 September 1939 the chief librarian was appointed food executive officer for the borough as well as chief librarian, and the reading room in the town hall was adapted for use as the food department. The free library committee were authorised to arrange for the conveyance of books and art treasures to safety in an emergency. Initially there was a decision not to hold lectures during the winter of 1939–40, but this resolution was rescinded later in the year. The borough surveyor was given the job of making sure that the library and museum building was protected. The Ministry of Information requested space for a photographic island display, where it would be seen by the vast majority of people, and permission was given for an exhibition of war photographs. Library services were extended to any American servicemen stationed in the area. During the war the public were reading more than ever. The shortage of paper caused a dearth in the number of books being published, and consequently stock deteriorated; it was almost impossible to have books bound during the war.

Joseph Pomfret worked in his dual role as chief librarian and food officer until his death on 5 February 1944—he had been borough librarian for sixteen years. He was held in high esteem by his colleagues, and had gained renown as a fluent lecturer on literary topics. His greatest achievement was the inauguration of the children's library in September 1935; he was unable to develop many of his plans because of the war. In between the death of Joseph Pomfret and the appointment of his successor, Raymond Irwin, the chief librarian of Lancashire County Library, acted in a supervisory capacity. In September 1945, Jane Downton, from Luton, was appointed as chief librarian.

The years immediately after the war saw a flurry of changes in organisation and development of services, mainly due to the new librarian, Jane Downton. The aim of the cataloguing department was to have books on the shelves within ten days of arrival at the library. A lending librarian was appointed to be not only a liaison between the chief librarian and the general public, but to be a 'guide, counsellor and friend to the borrowers'. To dispel some of the gloom of the library, it was redecorated with brighter colours, and lighting was replaced with fluorescent lights. The counter area was altered, to allow for two entrances and two exits. The expected decline in the number of issues after the war did not materialise at the Harris—issues continued in the few years after the war to be over 450,000. In her first annual report, Jane Downton's look into the future had an almost Churchillian ring about it: 'we are moving in the right direction but it will take us at least another four years of

The re-organised lending library in the years following the war. The library was redecorated and fluorescent lights fitted to give a brighter appearance.
(Courtesy of *Lancashire Evening Post*.)

unremitting toil and ceaseless care to give Preston the place to which her prestige and history entitles her'.[1] Another innovation at this time was the Book Week, in conjunction with the National Book League, held in the children's library from 25 November until 14 December 1946; the attendance of over ten thousand people gave expression to its popularity. The National Book League offered an exhibition 'Children's Books of Yesteryear'. The book week and exhibition became an annual event at the library for many years. Some of the books popular around this time were *The Gathering Storm* by Winston Churchill—the first volume of his memoirs of the Second World War; and Field Marshall Montgomery's *From Alamein to the Sangro*; there was also a demand for books on the colonies and emigration.

In the early 1950s, the music section was overhauled and enlarged. The most popular book of the time was Nevil Shute's *A Town Like Alice*, and war stories were still popular. The library was cooperating with the WEA and schools, and took every opportunity to link library services with the activities of the towns-people. The readers' advisory service was developed, and a new information desk was set up in the centre of the lending library in the mid 1950s.

The enquiry desk in the lending library in 1993. The computer system gives online access to a county-wide catalogue and is also capable of issuing books.

In 1953–54, the need was again expressed for branch libraries to relieve the pressure on the central library, and the new branch library at Ribbleton was opened on 29 March, 1954. Preston Borough took over the service at Ingol from the Lancashire County Library on 1 April 1956. The most heavily reserved book of the year was Sir John Hunt's *The Ascent of Everest*; books on space travel and the coronation were also popular.

A major change in the control of the library occurred in 1974, when the Local Government Act of 1972 came into force—control passed from the borough to the Lancashire County Council; control of the museum and art gallery remained with Preston Borough Council. It gave the opportunity for the Harris library to become part of a much larger organisation, with all the advantages of inter-library lending on a scale unknown previously, and access to services on a county-wide basis. The key to this was a comprehensive, shared catalogue for the county, which became available within about two years. In 1985, a new computer system was introduced which gave not only immediate, online access to a county-wide catalogue, but also had the capability of issuing and returning books, thus making obsolete the system of tickets and book cards which had been in existence since the early 1920s.

By 1976, the size of the library service in Preston had grown enormously since the war, and now included not only the services at the Harris library itself, but five branch libraries at Ribbleton, Ingol, Savick, Sharoe Green and Garstang Road, a mobile library, services to hospitals, homes for the elderly, and the prison; the issues for all these service points in 1976 totalled 1,460,535—three times the immediate post-war figure; in 1991/92, this figure was 1,552,982, excluding loans of videos, cassettes, records and compact discs, which would bring the total to approximately 1,648,000.

One of the most popular novelists in recent years has been Catherine Cookson, her most sought-after book in 1992/3 being *The Whip*. The only title issued more often than this was *The Storyteller* by Harold Robbins. Current non-fiction favourites include *Diana: her true story* by Andrew Morton and *Some Other Rainbow* by John McCarthy and Jill Morrell. *King Lear* was the most popular video loaned in 1992/3, while in the music library the highest issues in compact discs were for Pink Floyd's *Wish you were here*, closely followed by the Beatles' *Sgt. Pepper's Lonely Hearts Club Band*.

'A TRUE UNIVERSITY OF INSTRUCTION FOR OUR YOUTH'

THE JUNIOR LIBRARY, situated on the ground floor between the lending library and the library's administrative offices on the Harris Street side of the building, is light, modern, and attractive, and though understandably quiet during school time, is bursting at the seams on Saturdays. The staff make great efforts to interest young people in reading and creative work, not only in day to day contact, but by other means, some very well established, such as the magazine published twice a year. The children's library was opened on 23 September 1935, when the general news and reading room was transferred to the town hall to make room for it. By 1939 nearly 4,000 young people were registered as borrowers, and 57,606 books were issued in that year; by 1948, both these figures had more than doubled.

A very popular innovation in 1947 was the 'Story Hour'; for the first story hour, on 12 February 1947, 125 children attended, and on 12 March there were 210! As this number was too great to cater for adequately, it was decided to hold the story hour every week, and limit the numbers attending. The story hour was very popular for many years; but gradually, owing to several factors such as the establishment of branch libraries, some with their own story times, and the advent of television, the numbers attending story hour at the Harris library declined. Story hours were discontinued, except for holidays, but a story time for the under-fives was introduced two years ago.

Children's 'Story Hour' with Miss Hargreaves in 1947, the year the sessions began. These proved very popular, with over 200 children attending on some occasions.
(Courtesy of the *Lancashire Evening Post*.)

Many young Prestonians have had the pleasure of reading and contributing to the children's magazine published by the Harris library. The first *Children's Library Magazine* was published in November 1951, and was published thereafter three times a year until 1976, when the number of issues was reduced to two, which is still the case today. The magazine was renamed *Contact* for the summer edition 1980. The magazine is the children's own book, written by themselves, including short stories, poems, articles, book reviews, pets' corner amongst other things; a poem from the very first edition was 'My Dolly', by Barbara Begg, aged nine

> I have a little dolly,
> It's very, very old
> I left it in the rain one day
> And then it caught a cold.
>
> My Mummy hung it out to dry
> Its cold has really gone.
> I cannot tell you any more,
> Because it's half past one.

Several attempts have been made over the years to provide special services for adolescents. In March 1952 a book discussion group was formed for this age group; and a youth library for fifteen-to-twenty-year-olds was opened by the Guild mayoress on 26 January 1953. During the rest of the decade issues were around sixteen thousand per annum, but it was recognised that it was a difficult age group to interest and cater for and it ceased in 1972. A small collection of books for teenagers was set up in the adult lending library seven years ago.

One of the Harris's special collections is that of John Spencer, a local historian, linguist and book collector. For the 1947 book exhibition held at the library, John Spencer loaned around three hundred volumes for display, and later donated the collection to the library; on the 26 October 1950 he presented to the library his collection relating to Francis Thompson, including six original manuscripts and about one hundred volumes. Further donations of local books were made by John Spencer before his death in December 1952. There has been a continuing interest in the children's books from the Spencer collection locally, nationally and internationally.

The school library service within the Preston district serves nearly seventy schools, and in 1991 nearly five hundred sets of project loans were borrowed by schools. The library and museum's contact with schools has a long history, the first loans to elementary schools being made in 1897, when collections of photographs were loaned out from the museum; a few years later about two hundred pictures were also being circulated around local schools. By 1912 books were being loaned to secondary schools, and there may have been an early attempt in 1918 to establish school libraries, an attempt which turned out to be short-lived. By 1926, with the central lending library becoming very busy, the free library committee agreed jointly with the education committee to issue books through school libraries; this helped to relieve the situation in the lending library. Fifty boxes of books were prepared and loaned out to schools. The schools library service has continued ever since.

After local government reorganisation in 1974, the service continued, under the Lancashire County Council, and the number of schools served within the Preston district has continued to grow, from 23 in 1976 to 63 in 1991—the school library service operates in every primary school in the district. From April 1988, the base for the school library service was relocated to Lancashire County Library headquarters in Corporation Street, and project loan stock of the Harris was integrated with stock from headquarters.

Over the years the children's library has used many activities to interest children in literature, to stimulate their minds into creative endeavour and to broaden their minds, for instance: contacts were made with children in Preston,

Victoria, Australia in 1947–8; a music section was added to the children's library in 1953–54; and the ninth annual book exhibition in 1954 was devoted to children's books, with Geoffrey Trease opening the exhibition. From October 1980 a children's book week has been held, the one in 1991 being staged in the rural setting of Myerscough College and including displays of books, visits by authors of children's books and live theatre.

SPECIAL SERVICES

ONE CORNER OF THE LENDING LIBRARY has been specially designed for visually impaired people. Here the library service harnesses the latest technology to provide information in a suitable format for their use. From printed text it is possible to produce either speech, tape recordings, braille or large print copies of original documents; most clients require either tapes, braille or large print, as these can be easily taken home and used there. The equipment in use consists of a Kurzweil personal reading machine, a microcomputer, a braille machine, laser printer and a machine for magnifying text, pictures and small objects. The services provided by this unit are complementary to the many services already existing for the visually impaired, such as large print books, 'talking books', 'talking newspapers', music on cassette, record or compact disc, and children's book/cassette sets.

Works printed in braille for the blind were introduced in the Harris library ninety years ago; it seems that the work of issuing the books was given to a local blind society. In 1921, issuing braille books was taken over by the library, which was receiving consignments of books from the National Library for the Blind. Issues of books in that year were only 63, but by 1939 the figure had risen considerably to 773. In the years immediately after the war, however, issues were about a third of this figure; the main reasons for this probably being that readers were more likely to receive books direct to their homes from the National Library for the Blind, and from 1935 'talking books' were available, first on records and later on tapes, from the British Talking Book Service for the Blind, operating under the aegis of the Royal National Institute for the Blind. The Kurzweil personal reading machine and related equipment were introduced in 1989. The library service is continuing its long tradition of service to the visually impaired.

As part of its attempts to reach out to those unable to visit the library in person, the Harris library inaugurated the hospital library service on 10 November 1949. Initially service was provided to the Preston Royal Infirmary; this was soon extended to The Willows, the isolation hospital and The Chestnuts. The service was further extended in October 1951 to the civic hostel, Fulwood. By

1956 over twenty thousand books per year were being issued to the hospitals
and hostels. Service extended to the new Royal Preston Hospital in 1980, but
was taken over by the Preston health authority in 1986. The supply of books to
sheltered houses was rationalised in 1977 under the 'Shelbex' scheme, when nine
sheltered homes were being served. For the last ten years the people in these
homes have been using the services of the mobile library.

People housebound in their own homes and in homes for the elderly receive
an individual service from the library, each person being visited once a fortnight
by a member of the library staff. Currently about 140 people benefit from this
service.

About a third of convicted prisoners and those on trial and remand at HM
Prison, Preston, regularly make use of the library service provided for them at
the prison from the Harris library. In 1948, the Harris library was invited by
the Prison Commissioners to administer the library at the prison; the service
was inaugurated in 1948; Richard Watson, the assistant-in-charge, became a
registered prison visitor. The service has always been well-used; in the first year
over 10,000 books were issued; this had risen to 61,664 by 1953, reaching a peak
of over 116,000 in 1979—more than from three of the regular branch libraries
at the time. The information requested by prisoners is wide in scope and goes
far beyond light reading; many require advanced texts, journal articles and such
like, to further their research for degrees and other advanced study, although it
was noted in 1953 that a popular request was Paul Brickhill's *The Great Escape*!

For well over forty years Preston has enjoyed the advantages of an urban
mobile library—to reach the parts other libraries cannot reach! The 'travelling
library', as it was known initially, made its debut on 20 September 1948; borough
librarian Jane Downton saw it as 'a temporary, post-war measure' to meet the
needs of an ever increasing population living away from the centre of Preston.

The ethnic services section of the lending library in 1988. This service expanded rapidly during the 1980s when a special librarian was appointed. (Courtesy of Marjorie Amriding.)

Preston Borough Transport Department converted a 1932 Leyland single-decker rear entry bus into a mobile library. 'Bertie' the travelling library was on the road every day, visiting each of six sites three times in a week. In 1953 it issued 153,480 books, equal to nearly a third of the books issued from the main central lending library. By 1958 it was visiting ten sites. After the opening of the new branch library at Ingol in August 1981, the mobile library's hours were reduced, and then the service discontinued altogether. However the service was reinstated five months later, after a public outcry, and by 1985 issues were again over 100,000 per year.

The library, sensitive to the needs of ethnic groups in the area, has over the years provided literature in a number of languages. In 1957 Polish literature was being borrowed from the Polish Research Centre in London; later, collections of books in Urdu and Gujerati were held, as were books supporting the Adult Literacy Scheme. By 1980 books in Urdu, Bengali, Gujerati, Hindi and Punjabi were being well used, and during the 1980s there was a further expansion of stock, helped by urban aid funds, to include in addition items in Vietnamese and Afro-Caribbean languages. This aspect of the service has been developed further by the appointment of an ethnic services librarian who works in the community, promoting the library's services at cultural events, in community and education centres, and working with specialist organisations.

REFERENCE LIBRARY

THE REFERENCE AND INFORMATION SERVICE, like the other library departments in the Harris building, is part of a network of reference libraries throughout the Lancashire County Library and thus serves not only the people of Preston and its immediate surrounds, but also of the wider county, and indeed has many enquiries from other parts of the country and from abroad; currently, about 45,000 enquiries are dealt with each year by staff, and about 100,000 people actually visited the reference department in the year ending March 1993. There is a vast amount of information available, and people use the resources for a wide variety of reasons—for educational study and research, for research relating to work, for help in the problems of daily life, for information relating to health and medicine, for local information about Preston, for researching family history, and for many other purposes. The resources available to these users are wide and not confined within the building—although much information is still in printed form, such as books, newspapers and periodicals, many sources are now on microfilm or microfiche, and computers are used not only to look at the library's own catalogue, but to receive instantaneous information from computers in other parts of the country and indeed the world; the fax machine can transmit information in a matter of seconds; compact discs containing vast amounts of text are another source being used increasingly to find information for library users. The contrast could not be greater from the early years of the reference library's history when each volume used had to be requested—there

The reference library in 1993. Currently around 45,000 enquiries are dealt with each year, not only from the Preston area but from other parts of the country and abroad.

The reference library in the 1930s, a time which saw its increased usage as a result of the depression.

was no helping yourself. In the first full year after its opening in 1896–7 just under 10,000 volumes were consulted; these had risen to 19,000 by 1905.

In their annual report in 1912, the free library committee voiced a feeling that echoes down the decades to the present day, even though the reference service is now busier than ever, 'Although the Committee are gratified by their knowledge of the fact that a large body of readers resort regularly to the Reference Library, they cannot but feel that the riches stored on its shelves might be much further utilised by the community'.[2]

The new Dewey decimal classification system was first introduced in the reference library in 1919, and was appreciated by the students, who were also allowed limited access to the shelves. This change was followed shortly by the introduction of catalogues on cards instead of in printed volumes; the effect of the changes was an increase in usage: in 1920 the annual usage of volumes was 14,536; this rose to 23,167 in 1922. As in the lending department, issues rose during the depression of the early 1930s, reaching nearly 25,000 by 1935.

From 1 October 1947, opening hours for the reference library were extended to 8.00 p.m., and on 1 January 1948, to 9.00 p.m.; it was well attended in the evening hours. In 1955 a microfilm reader was introduced, with microfilms of *The Times*, *Times Literary Supplement*, *Times Educational Supplement* and the Patent Office press mark index. From May 1969, construction of the fire escape began, and the iron spiral staircase which had been there since the building was constructed was 'banished'. From 20 March 1970, in order to create more room, some periodicals were removed to the GPO basement, as the forerunner to a general reorganisation of the reference library. Towards the end of March 1971, preparations were made for the installation of mobile shelving. At this time nearly five hundred newspaper and periodical titles were being received.

In 1992 the reference department was refurbished and almost all of the room made accessible to the users—echoing in some respects the move made in 1905 when it was reorganised so that the room 'might be devoted from end to end to the use of readers'; there the comparison ends, for the room today is bright and colourful, and resplendent with varied foliage, and armchairs, but still retaining the original walnut shelving and tables. Users today have access to almost all the shelves, and it is very busy—not only with personal visitors, but with over 800 telephone calls a month, and requests for information by letter and fax.

The Local Studies Collection is one of the most well-used areas of the reference library. By the end of the Second World War the library already had a nucleus of a local collection including local history books, maps, pamphlets and other material. Donations received over the years included those from John H. Spencer and the purchase of the Francis Thompson manuscripts, the latter being described as the most important event in the history of the Harris library. Francis Thompson was born at 7 Winckley Street, Preston on 16 December 1859; he lived in Preston up to the age of five. Early in 1955 the free library committee was given the opportunity of purchasing several manuscripts for £290. In June of that year they were offered the manuscript of *Sister Songs*, together with relevant letters, for £1,000. The Friends of National Libraries gave £50, and a public subscription was opened for the remainder which raised £819 16s. 1d. Mrs Olivia Sowerby, the owner, reduced the price to £900; the remainder was paid for from the Harris endowment.

In 1958 the Preston Scientific Society deposited their record and survey committee's photographic collection. Another donation in 1962 was a microfilm copy of a thesis on James Hibbert by Margaret Bowe. In addition, by 1960 there was a local societies' list being kept—there was and remains a great demand from library users for contacts in local societies and organisations, and for the last ten years this information has been kept on computer for easier updating. Today the library holds a large local studies collection on Preston and its

The Dr Shepherd Library in the Harris in the late 1890s. At that time readers had to be recommended by the mayor or an alderman.

surroundings and as well as books, pamphlets and journals in printed form, has census returns, parish registers, newspapers and other material on microfilm and microfiche. About 25 per cent of all enquiries in this department are for local information.

The commercial and technical section of the reference library is one of its most important features. It was back in 1918, the same year as Leeds established their commercial and technical library, that a proposal was put to the free library committee to establish one in Preston; the matter was deferred, the committee stating that 'we have a definite public for this type of work and it is a suggestion to be borne in mind when future policy is formulated'. There has always been a demand for commercial and technical information; links were established with the Preston Chamber of Commerce in 1949. In 1950, the directory collection was moved from the newsroom to the reference library, and the scope of the commercial section was widened by the addition of several city and town directories. In 1954, as part of the North Western Regional Library Bureau's subject specialisation scheme, Preston became responsible for purchasing books on all aspects of electricity, aeronautics, aerodynamics and types of painting— earlier it was said that the 'reference library has always had a reputation for its collection of copiously and finely illustrated books on individual artists and schools of painting'. More use was being made of the library by local firms.

Early in the 1960s the Preston commercial and technical information service was created, a cooperative local scheme between twenty-four libraries and firms each willing to lend, mainly periodicals, to each other; this was sponsored by the Harris library; but it gradually faded out.

When the Lancashire County Library took over responsibility for all libraries in the county in 1974, there was a commercial and technical library in library headquarters in Corporation Street in Preston. As an economy measure in 1981 this was closed down and the resources transferred to the Harris reference library. About 25 per cent of all enquiries are for commercial and technical information; a large number of directories are held, three series of market reports, Infocheck reports giving detailed financial information on over 300,000 companies, and computer access to Companies House and many other electronic sources of commercial and technical information.

Dr Shepherd's library had been part of the reference library since it opened in 1895, the first users having to be recommended by the mayor or an alderman. This library was frequently consulted but lacked a satisfactory catalogue. In 1961 an exhibition was staged to celebrate the bi-centenary of the death of Richard Shepherd. The Shepherd Library was moved in 1982 down to the basement to permit the market square end of the room to be opened up to users and to allow for more open access shelving.

NOTES

1. Harris Public Library Annual Report, 1947.
2. Harris Free Library and Museum, 33rd Annual Report, 1912.

7

Museum and Art Gallery in the Twentieth Century

THE HARRIS ART GALLERY is renowned for its collection of the works of nineteenth-century British artists whose paintings were collected on a grand scale by local man Richard Newsham and bequeathed to the town after his death in 1883. Through a long-standing association with the Contemporary Arts Society, and with help from the Arts Council of Great Britain and Preston Borough Council, the practice of collecting contemporary paintings has continued, even if the paintings are somewhat different from the more traditional ones of the nineteenth century, themes such as landscape, portraiture and the classical tradition are still reflected in contemporary purchases; further help in purchasing modern works is given by the Victoria and Albert Museum purchase grant fund, the Granada Foundation, and the Friends of the Harris; between 1985 and 1992 art works to the value of £200,000 were added to collections via the Contemporary Art Purchase Scheme. The museum and art gallery uses a modern in-house MODES (Museum Object Data Entry System) computer system, making the storage and retrieval of details of all its works of art and museum objects much more comprehensive; and makes use of modern technology to enhance the museum displays in the building. The principal museum collections, apart from a large display on the 'Story of Preston', are of glass, ceramics, costume, toys and dolls. The museum and art gallery encourage community involvement in such activities as oral history projects, by lending exhibits and encouraging the making of artwork; and the Community Gallery is used for a variety of exhibitions by local organisations.

Art Gallery

IN THIS CENTENARY YEAR, the bright and spacious art gallery on the south side of the second floor is appropriately housing an exhibition of paintings purchased

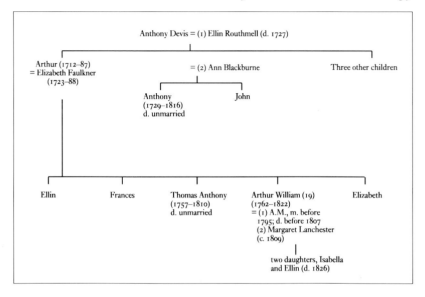

The Devis family tree.

for the Harris building over the last one hundred years, entitled '10 × 10 Years of New Art', including, Walter Osbourne's *Summer Time* purchased in 1901, George Spencer Watson's *Nude* which evoked much protest and controversy when it was purchased in 1927, Charles Spencelayh's *Why War?*, purchased in the year the Second World War broke out, Anthony Devas' *At the Couturier* (1955), and Augustus John's *Dorelia*, purchased in 1959—one of the last pictures purchased by the curator and art director, Sydney Paviere, before he retired. A recent exhibition in this centenary year displayed seventeenth- and eighteenth-century art, including Arthur William Devis' *Portrait of an Actor*, paintings by Jan Van Os (1744–1808), and others by Thomas Anthony Devis (1757–1810) and a self-portrait by Arthur Devis (1712–1787). In the original plans, this gallery housed the natural history and physics exhibits.

The four artists in the Devis family are important to Preston and over the years the art gallery has collected a large number of their works. Thomas Anthony Devis and his brother Arthur William were sons of Arthur Devis; Anthony Devis was Arthur's half-brother. Both Anthony Devis and Arthur Devis were born in Preston.

The first exhibition in the Harris of the work of the Devis family was in March 1937. Although Arthur Devis had been noted for his portraits, the work of the family as a whole had been largely unknown to the general public up to this time. Two previously unknown portraits, one by Arthur and the other by Arthur William, were exhibited along with other pictures from Lytham Hall in December 1955. To celebrate the centenary of the Newsham bequest, the Harris staged an exhibition of about sixty paintings by Arthur Devis from October to 12 November 1983, entitled 'Polite Society: Portraits of the English Country Gentleman and his Family'; it was very pleasing for the town that the exhibition then moved to the National Portrait Gallery later in that year. On the recently built mezzanine floor at the east end of the second floor, space is set aside for exhibitions of water-colours, and a recent exhibition showed paintings by Anthony Devis (1729–1816), entitled 'A Picturesque Traveller'; he was famous for landscape painting and the exhibition shows many paintings of different parts of the country, including scenes of the Lake District, Lancashire, Wales and even as far south as Sussex, with his *Beachy Head from Bexhill* in watercolour and pen.

On the north side of this floor, set aside for special exhibitions, and in the original conception of the building to be the fine art gallery, there was housed recently an exhibition by Preston Art Society; this exhibiting of local artists' work has been important since the early days of the gallery. The central balcony of this floor also acts as an art gallery, containing such paintings as *In the Bey's Garden*, by John Frederick Lewis (1805–1876), a picture which is part of the Newsham collection and which has been exhibited elsewhere many times. It was shown at the British Empire Exhibition in 1924–5. This gallery features other examples from the Newsham bequest and also the Vaughan bequest, such as *Cordelia Disinherited* by John Roger Herbert (1810–1890).

The staircase between the first and second floors is used as a picture gallery; the current exhibition, 'British Artists Abroad', includes *Antwerp Cathedral* by David Roberts, which again is part of the Newsham collection. It was first decided to use the staircase for displaying pictures and photographs in 1901 and for many years portraits of prominent people of Preston could be seen here; these were men who 'have added lustre or knowledge to the world in the sphere of their various activities';[1] the decision to form this collection was first made in 1926 and the exhibition was in place before 1932, when some of the portraits displayed were: Sir Richard Arkwright, Joseph Livesey, Dr Richard Shepherd, and Revd Robert Harris. The picture of Sir Richard Arkwright was painted by William Simm, the assistant art director, who was allowed to visit London in 1928 to complete a copy of Arkwright's portrait in the National Portrait Gallery. In 1935 the idea was first proposed of establishing a gallery of portraits of Guild mayors and honorary freemen of the borough, and where these portraits did not already exist eminent artists should be commissioned to execute the paintings; one of the artists was William Simm. Among the portraits produced were those of Samuel Horrocks MP, and Samuel Horrocks, Guild mayor in 1842. A portrait of Sir William Ascroft by R. E. Morrison was donated by William Ascroft's son to go with the portraits of Prestonians exhibited in the art gallery.

There has been a long tradition of exhibiting work by local artists on the walls of the staircase between the ground and first floors. Recently, an 'Art in Lancashire' display showed work which included James Ferguson's *Ribble from Stanley Terrace*, and paintings by Arthur Devis and Anthony Devis; in the 1932 summary guide it was recorded that there were a number of watercolours, etchings, lithographs and drawings depicting Preston and the neighbourhood, including drawings by Edwin Beattie, who was born in Liverpool but lived some time in Preston. On this staircase also can be seen the memorial to those local men who died during the First World War. The stone war memorial panels were carved about 1927, it is said by a deaf and dumb stonemason who worked at night to avoid interfering with visitors during the day. The foreman caretaker of the time, John Blanchflower, recalled later his nights spent looking after the building, the only sound being the monotonous chip and crack of the stonemason's chisel. He also recalled the time a new member of staff working late was terrified by a man in the cellars; it turned out to be the museum's black baboon, waiting to be cleaned!

The art gallery has benefited greatly over the years from bequests made to it, and from purchases made both locally and from exhibitions held in the large galleries in London, particularly the Royal Academy. As previously mentioned, Richard Newsham bequeathed paintings and other art treasures to the corporation in 1883. After initially being housed in the guild hall, these paintings were moved to the Harris building in time for the opening of the museum and art section to the public on 1 January 1896—these paintings of early nineteenth-century British artists thus forming a nucleus of a fine arts collection which has grown considerably since that time from further bequests and many purchases. To complement the collection, there was in 1901 a loan from the Victoria and Albert of 300 pictures illustrating the rise and progress of the British School of Painting. In the same year, a bequest of six paintings was received from the late Joseph Sumner, and two years later the Dewhurst bequest; other bequests received include Fearnside, Vaughan, and Sandby. Revd John Park Haslam, of Ambleside, bequeathed a collection of English water-colours in 1925, and also money for the furtherance of watercolour painting, and a copy of the Kelmscott edition of Chaucer's poems.

The art gallery prior to 1926 showing the permanent collection of paintings held at that time.
(Courtesy of the Harris Museum and Art Gallery.)

*The Egyptian gallery, high up in the lantern of the building, showing the murals by John Somerscales
and the Assyrian bas-reliefs.*

In the Egyptian gallery high up in the lantern of the building, as well as the Assyrian bas-reliefs already alluded to, are to be found murals painted by John Somerscales. In October 1908, he was commissioned to visit Egypt to make drawings of the ancient temples and other buildings with a view to painting these murals to illustrate ancient Egyptian art. On his return, his collection of water colours of the pyramids and the temples of Abydos, Karnak, Korn Ombo and Philae were put on exhibition in the lecture room. These murals took the artist four years to complete. After this, he painted a frieze for the sculpture gallery on the first floor based on the story of the reliefs surrounding the Choragic Monument of Lysicrates at Athens, and on the second floor, beneath the Parthenon frieze, he painted murals showing a range of Greek architectural remains, including a view of the Acropolis and the Temple of Theseus at Athens, and the ruins of the Temple of Venus on the ancient site of the town of Aphrodisias in Asia Minor; neither of these murals is extant. In 1913, the panelled decoration of the staircase up to the Egyptian gallery was begun, under the direction of John Somerscales, the subjects being derived from illustrations of the Ancient Egyptian 'Book of the Dead'.

Some of the acquisitions of pictures up to the time of the retirement of William Barton in 1925 included, *The Eleventh Hour, the Eleventh Day, of the Eleventh Month, 1918* by W. P. Day which is currently on display; *A September Morning in the Hebrides* by John Menzies; *German Scuttling at Scapa Flow* by Bernard F. Gribble; *Early Morning, Les Baux, Provence* by Sir H. Hughes Stanton; and a painting by Stanhope Forbes purchased from the Royal Academy entitled *On the Bridge*. Among some of the notable pictures loaned to the Harris during this period were Constable's *On the Stour* and Turner's *Venice*, loaned by Thomas Miller of Singleton Park.

William Bright Barton had been curator and art director since the infancy of the Harris Museum and Art Gallery, and after the retirement of William Bramwell as chief librarian in 1916, he added that post to his responsibilities. After his retirement in 1925, Sidney H. Paviere, an artist himself, was appointed art director and curator, taking up his post on 4 January 1926.

One of the first major decisions made after Sydney Paviere became art director was to institute the exhibition of Lancashire artists, which until recently was an annual event at the Harris; not only did this give local artists an opportunity to display their work, but also the Harris has over the years enhanced its own collection by making purchases from the exhibition—one of the first to be purchased was a picture entitled *Porch of St Mary the Virgin, Oxford* by a certain Sydney Paviere in 1926. This first Lancashire artists' exhibition was organised by the art section of the Preston Scientific Society and ran from 31 March until 28 April; there had previously been exhibitions of local artists' work, but these had been limited to artists in the Preston area. Among the exhibitors were Percy Lancaster from Southport, including his *Sawley Bridge* and *On the Kent*; Tom Anderton from Bamber Bridge with *Sunrise*; William Rathbone, art master at the Harris Institute, with a number of works including *Still Life* in monochrome. The exhibition was very popular and the work of many artists had to be turned away, either because of the low standard, or because of lack of exhibition space. At the opening ceremony Sidney Paviere urged that young people should be encouraged to visit the exhibition, and that the appreciation and practice of art should figure more prominently in their education. After the success of this first Lancashire artists' exhibition, it became an annual event and it was at the thirty-fourth Lancashire Art Exhibition in 1959 that Sidney Paviere announced his retirement; in that year he described the works exhibited as 'essentially the product of "Sunday painters"—amateurs who find delight in capturing a favourite scene or expressing an idea without claiming to be great artists'.

One of the more unusual requests made in 1935 was for permission for Jackatoon Film Company Ltd of Lancaster and London to film five pictures in the art gallery for incorporation into an educational film.

In 1934 a passenger lift was installed to make life easier both for visitors to the building and for transporting art works, books and other materials. In 1933 a radio gramophone was purchased for use with lectures for £17—lectures were held at this time on the first floor in what is now the 'Story of Preston' room.

Among the donations received and purchases made in the period when Sydney Paviere was art director included one in 1928 from a Mrs Morris, daughter of Mr Barclay Clemesha, entitled *A Strong Breeze in the Channel* by Thomas Somerscales; an oil painting of Aloysius Smith ('Trader Horn') by John Park; *Battle of Preston* by Charles Cattermole; *A River Scene with Mansion Among the Trees* by Anthony Devis, donated by the Rt Hon. Sir Philip Sassoon; *In a Camden Hill Studio* by W. Russell Flint; two portraits by Anthony Devis, and one, *Albury House* by the same artist, donated by Dr Samuel Courtauld of London; *Oxford* by Anthony Devis; and twenty-seven oil paintings by Thomas Wade; *Portrait of a Parson* by Arthur Devis, purchased in 1935–6 for 125 guineas, and a self-portrait of the same artist painted around 1754; a portrait of Miss Ellin Devis by Arthur W. Devis (1762–1822); also the picture *Why War?* by Charles Spencelayh already referred to, bought on 15 May 1939. During the war there were purchases of *Wisteria* by Stanley Spencer, and from the Royal Academy *Pauline in the Yellow Dress* by James Gunn—this cost £1,000. The executors of the will of Lord Ribblesdale donated several paintings in 1944; and three years later eleven watercolours were donated by the war artists' advisory committee; by this time a room had been set aside for displaying the works of the Devis family.

SCULPTURE

IN THE CENTRAL GALLERY of the second floor, in addition to the paintings mentioned above, there are now sculptures such as *Mother and Child* by Albert Toft of the British School. In the early years of the building, this gallery was set aside for sculptures, some of these being reproductions of Greek and Roman statuary; these reproductions no longer exist. Sculptures can be found in the central areas of all three floors. On the first floor, including several with connections with the building, are bronze busts of Alderman Hibbert, by William Simm, purchased in 1934, and Richard Newsham, by the same artist, purchased in 1929. Further examples are of Alderman W. H. Woods, by E. Whitney-Smith (1910), and Pasteur—in a very thoughtful mood—from the French sculptor Antonin Carles; also here is to be found a very early acquisition—a bronze cast of Bologna's *Flying Mercury*. On the ground floor there are also several busts, including one of Miss Harris (Edmund Robert Harris's sister Ellen Elizabeth), by Rowland Rhodes; and one of the Revd Robert Harris, Edmund Robert's father, by Thomas Duckett, made around 1845. Gone are the reproductions of Greek, Roman and Renaissance figures which were introduced by the architect James Hibbert to complement the classical style of the building itself, for example Michelangelo's figure of David, which originally was the focal point of the central hall on the ground floor: these reproductions were still on display in 1932, but by 1948 were no

Photograph taken in the 1930s of the bust of the mythological 'Clytie' struggling out of her flower calyx, sculptured by George Watts (1817–1904). This remains a focal point at the top of the stairs leading to the art gallery.
(Courtesy of the Harris Museum and Art Gallery.)

A replica of the eastern gate of the baptistry of the Church of S Giovanni in Florence by Lorenzo Ghiberti has been on exhibit in the Harris building since its opening. The photograph shows one of the panels from the gate which, in all, depicts ten scenes from the Old Testament.

longer to be seen. The classical theme, however, is extended by contemporary works such as those by Stephen Cox, Dhruva Mistry and Calum Colvin, a theme which is also developed by nineteenth- and twentieth-century bronzes by artists like Frederick Leighton and Hamo Thorneycroft. There is also a pair of bronzes entitled *Discobolus* which are copies of statues found in Herculaneum in AD 1754, and the replica of the Renaissance eastern gate of the baptistry of the Church of S Giovanni in Florence by Lorenzo Ghiberti, described by Michelangelo as being worthy to be called 'The Gates of Paradise'—this shows ten scenes in gold from the Old Testament, with the exterior frame of the gate covered with flowers, plants and animals; the Ghiberti gate has formed part of the decoration of the Harris building for the whole of its existence.

Mention has been made of structural alterations providing mezzanine floors on the first and second floors; these alterations were part of several changes made in the 1980s to make the building more welcoming and to improve access for the disabled. Other alterations included the refurbishment of the education suite, and the remodelling of the entrance, with the addition of classically inspired artistic work by Ian Hamilton Finlay.

MUSEUM

FROM THE VERY FIRST, provision was made for natural history exhibits to be shown—James Hibbert allowed a whole gallery on the second floor for 'Natural History and Physics'; later, when the whole of this floor was given over to art galleries, the natural history collection was transferred to the north gallery of the first floor. In 1932 this collection comprised British and foreign birds, mammals, birds' eggs, and British lepidoptera. There were many donations over the years to this collection, including one in 1906 from Mr Jonathan H. Calvert, of Avenham Tower, of a collection of British birds; and in 1929 an offer from a Mr W. R. Moss of St Anne's volunteering to collect birds' eggs for the museum, free of charge! In 1933 the Frohawk collection of British bird skins, eggs and nests, and a collection of British butterflies, was purchased for £120. Of the mammals on show, the principal ones were the Koodoo bull, antelope, chamois, deer, giraffe, kangaroo and lion. The museum also received the Turner collection of shells. The natural history room was still there in 1948, but the museum no longer has a natural history section.

The exhibition cases on the first floor contain a large collection of fine glassware, mainly of the eighteenth and early nineteenth century; among the donations to this collection was glassware from the seventeenth to the nineteenth centuries from Mrs A. M. Taylor in 1945; there are also cases given over to ceramics, mainly English pottery and porcelain; much of this was part of a bequest from Mr Cedric Houghton in 1910. The identification, selection and cataloguing of the items were done by Bernard Rackham of the Victoria and Albert Museum; and he helped in providing a printed catalogue of the items in 1928; a separate room for displaying the Houghton bequest was opened on 31 January 1927. Further additions were made before 1948 by the children of Thomas Dewhurst, and by the Ada Watson bequest.

British coins from Anglo-Saxon times to the present, and tradesmen's tokens from the seventeenth, eighteenth and nineteenth centuries are held; these include some from the Cuerdale Hoard of silver coins from the tenth century. This hoard of silver coins, ingots and ornaments was discovered in 1840 in Cuerdale, near Preston, close to the River Ribble. As treasure trove, it became the property of the queen, who wished it to be disposed of in a manner which would further archaeological and numismatic science; and so the hoard was divided up and some coins sent to the British Museum and others to over 170 private collections and public institutions. In June 1961 a hoard of gold and

A museum display in the early years of the Harris. On the left are the two Bronze Age canoes which were found during the excavations of the Ribble dock. Only one survives today and it is on display in the 'Story of Preston' exhibition.

silver coins dating from the sixteenth and seventeenth centuries was discovered at St Annes, and this was deposited in the Harris museum. Among the medals held by the museum are the Seringapatum Medal of 1799, issued by the East India Company who took part in the capture of Seringapatum.

There are exhibits of silver card cases, scent bottles, English and continental gold and silver ware, examples of bronzes from Japan, enamel work, including Chinese and Japanese cloisonne, English Battersea and South Staffordshire patch boxes (part of the Houghton bequest), watches with enamel cases and French enamels. On the ground floor is the Global Clock—this is eighteenth-century French, purchased from the Lowther Castle sale by Mr Ewart Bradshaw and given to the museum in 1947; the globe is supported by bronze figures of boys, and the whole stands on a Shap granite pedestal.

Many donations of costume have been made since 1939, including Edwardian costume by Dr Joan Evans, and eighteenth- and nineteenth-century costume by Sir Roger and Lady Hulton. A collection of dolls, toys and games started in 1939 and about the same time valentines and greetings cards were being accumulated.

Foucault's pendulum was installed in 1909 by George J. Gibbs, the honorary curator of the Preston Observatory; the wire is about 35 metres (115') long, and the bob weighs about 13.5 kilograms (30 lbs); it gives evidence for the rotation of the earth. Jean Bernard Leon Foucault (1819–1868) was awarded the cross of the Legion of Honour in 1851 for his pendulum experiment, which he tried out first at home, then in the Paris Observatory and then in the Pantheon in Paris, after which time it was repeated in many parts of the world. Some yeasrs ago the pendulum was out of action for a time, the original wire having broken, but it was reinstated for the Preston Guild of 1992, when the 'first swing' was performed appropriately by Howard Stableford of the BBC's *Tomorrow's World* on 12 June of that year.

STORY OF PRESTON

ON ENTERING THE NORTH GALLERY of the first floor today to see the 'Story of Preston' exhibition, one encounters an environment very different from the lofty rooms with large windows characteristic of the other rooms on the ground and first floors; a mezzanine floor was constructed here recently, so the lower part is given over to 'The Story of Preston', while the upper storey is used as the social history exhibition gallery. The lower gallery brings together modern means of communicating information to the visitor, such as videos and accompanying music to illustrate the history of Preston and its surrounding district from pre-historic times until today. The exhibition is updated and refreshed from time to time as new information and exhibits are acquired.

The bed of the Ribble has been the scene for discoveries of pre-historic and Bronze age remains, such as axe-heads and stone hammers, and two canoes which date back to the Bronze Age found in the Ribble dock excavations. Only one of these survives. The Bronze Age is further represented by timber posts and collared urns from the Bleasdale Circle on Fairsnape Fell; this was a centre for religious worship as part of a farmers' settlement of about 1700 BC, where the farmers lived by herding cattle and growing crops.

Other exhibits which came into the museum's possession as a result of the dock excavations 1884–8 are red deer antlers and skulls of humans, oxen and pilot whales. The Roman occupation of the area, particularly of Walton and Ribchester, strategically placed on the Ribble on the route to the north, is illustrated by Samian ware, a cavalryman's helmet and coins from the period 114–238 AD which were discovered at Kirkham in 1936.

The origin of Preston is intimately connected with the Anglo-Saxon bishop St Wilfrid, who was granted land near the Ribble in about 670 AD; the name

The 'Story of Preston' uses videos and accompanying music as well as exhibits to illustrate the history of the town from prehistoric times to the present day.

'Priest's Town' was given to the settlement in reference to the monks established there, and it is from this name, through various derivatives over the centuries, that we get the name 'Preston'. Religion has always played an important part in the life of the town and in medieval times, in addition to the parish church, there was a Franciscan friary, from which the present Friargate gets its name, and the museum exhibits a holy water stoup and figure from this friary.

Viking art is illustrated by gilt bronze tortoise brooches discovered in 1822 at Claughton Hall near Garstang. The timber motte and bailey castle at Penwortham has provided examples of Norman bolts, keys and nails, and Preston itself had due mention in the Domesday Book. Royal charters are an important part of the town's heritage and copies of some of the charters are exhibited, as is a fourteenth-century 'custumal', which is the most complete list of rights and privileges held by the burgesses of Preston—including 'That they may have a Gild Merchant'. Guilds have been held from 1328, and from 1542 have been held every twenty years, the most recent being in 1992. The 1397 Guild Roll of tradesmen entitled to belong to one of the trade guilds is displayed.

Coins of the Civil War period from the St Annes hoard discovered in 1961 form part of the display, and the Battle of Preston of 1648, on Ribbleton Moor, is recalled by a sword and cannon ball discovered on the site. Some of the trades and industries of the town are illustrated by medieval pottery, a model of the water frame invented by one of Preston's famous sons, Richard Arkwright, items from the Horrocks family of cotton manufacturers, a weaving loom, and a display of Preston's shipping heritage.

The Devis family of painters already alluded to form part of the rich tapestry of the town's story and the exhibition illustrates their contribution to the area's artistic heritage. Among the many other aspects of the town's history illustrated are education, the Preston Guild, developments in local government, transport, the temperance movement, and some of the museum's collection of dolls form part of the display in a mock-up of a draper's shop.

The room which houses this exhibition reminds one of the classical theme that was so important at the building's inception, for at the end of it one of the windows was replaced in 1904 by a modern stained glass, by Henry Holiday, with an ancient theme—the literature, science and arts of Ancient Greece, depicting Aeschylus, Sophocles, Aristotle, Pythagoras, Euclid and many other Greek immortals.

NOTES

1. *Harris Museum and Art Gallery: Summary Guide* (Preston, 1932), p. 30.

Epilogue

OR ONE HUNDRED YEARS the Harris has fulfilled its role in the educational and recreational life of the people of Preston and beyond, being faithful to its dedication to 'literature, arts and sciences'. The Harris is more than this, however; it has regularly formed the backdrop to important local events, particularly after the destruction by fire and subsequent removal of the town hall. As the town's most distinguished building, it has figured in such events as the return of the local regiments in 1919, the celebrations at the winning of the FA Cup by Preston North End in 1938, the visit by the Queen and the Duke of Edinburgh in April 1955 when it was bedecked with bunting, and the celebrations of the Guild Merchant—the most recent of which was in 1992 when the Guild, now a truly international event, was proclaimed from the steps of the Harris, which itself has an international reputation in the field of learning.

And so to the future! The Harris building often echoes to the sound of classes of excited children, wending their way through the galleries, library and museum departments, peering precariously over balustrades, watching videos in the library, participating in activities in the museum's community gallery, thus widening their horizons and hopefully forming habits of enquiry and observation that will remain with them for a lifetime. It is to such as these that the Harris will be entrusted in the years of its second century.

The Harris in its centenary year, 1993, remains the most imposing building in the town.

CHRONOLOGY

1694   Richard Shepherd born near Kendal.

1712   Arthur Devis born in Preston.

1729   Anthony Devis born in Preston.

1761   Dr Richard Shepherd died, bequeathing his library to the town.

1764   Robert Harris christened in Clitheroe (4 March).

1797   Robert Harris appointed vicar of St George's Preston (December).

1798   Richard Newsham born in Preston (May).

1803   Edmund Robert Harris born (6 September).

1833   James Hibbert christened in Preston (15 February).

1854   First attempts in Preston towards adopting Public Libraries Act (1854–9).

1862   Robert Harris died (6 January).

1869   Edmund Robert Harris appointed Prothonotary and Associate for Lancashire.

1870   Education Act.

1877   Edmund Robert Harris died (27 May).
        Committee appointed to consider establishing a public library in Preston (27 September).

1878   A public meeting of ratepayers agrees that a public library be established (29 January).
        William Bramhall appointed Librarian (October).

1879   Public lending library, news and reading room opened in the town hall (1 January).
        Council approved a report for the foundation of a free public library and museum in association with the trustees of Edmund Robert Harris (1 May).
        William Bramhall resigned as Librarian; succeeded by William Storey Bramwell (August).

1880   Miss Margaret Barton appointed Curator of the museum (29 April).
        Museum opened in Cross Street (1 May).
        Preston Improvement Act 1880 receives royal assent (2 August).

1882   Revd Jonathan Shortt appointed Honorary Curator of museum (May).
        Foundation stone laid for the Harris Free Public Library and Museum (5 September).

1883   Building work commenced on the Harris Free Public Library and Museum (October).
        Richard Newsham bequest of paintings made to corporation (December).

1884   Newsham collection opened to the public in Guild Hall (May).

1886   Edwin Roscoe Mullins contracted to produce pedimental sculpture *The Age of Pericles*.

1891   Death of Miss Margaret Barton; succeeded as Curator by Thomas Busfield (March).

1893   Ceremonial opening of Harris Free Public Library and Museum by the Earl of Derby (26 October).

1894   Lending library, news room and reading room of the Harris opened to the public (1 January).

1895   Dr Shepherd Library reopened in Harris (8 April).
        Reference library opened.
        William Bright Barton appointed Art Director and Curator.

1896   Museum, picture and sculpture galleries opened to the public (1 January).

1898   James Hibbert moved to London to live.

1903   James Hibbert died in Croydon.

1909   Foucault's Pendulum installed.

1916   William Storey Bramwell retired as Librarian (February).

1917   William Bright Barton assumes additional appointment as Chief Librarian.

1923   'Open access' system introduced in lending library.

1925   William Bright Barton retired. Frank Helliwell appointed Chief Librarian (1 April).

1926   Sidney H. Paviere begins appointment as Art Director and Curator (4 January).
        First Lancashire Artists' Exhibition (March–April).

1928   Frank Helliwell resigned (January); succeeded by Joseph Pomfret (12 September).

1935   Childrens' library opened in Harris (23 September).

1944   Joseph Pomfret died (5 February).

1945   Jane Downton appointed Chief Librarian (September).

1947   John H. Spencer makes first donation of books to Harris.

1948   Prison library service inaugurated.
        Mobile library service instituted (20 September).

1949   Hospital library service inaugurated (10 November).

1953   Youth library opened in Harris (26 January).

1955   Francis Thompson manuscripts purchased for Harris.

1959   Sidney Paviere retired; succeeded as Art Director and Curator by Helena Gibbon
        (October).

1972   Jane Downton retired (January); succeeded by James Brown (31 January).
        Gillian Tresidder appointed Art Director and Curator (May).

1974   Local Government Act 1972 came into force; control of library service passed to
        Lancashire County Council (1 April).
        James Brown became Deputy County Librarian; Richard Watson appointed District
        Librarian for Preston (1 April).

1978   Michael Cross appointed Assistant Director of Leisure and Amenities (Museum and
        Arts) (September).

1979   Richard Watson retired; succeeded by Michael Curtis (September).

1983   Michael Curtis became Assistant County Librarian; succeeded as District Librarian by
        Mena Williams (1 May).

1985   Geac online computer system introduced into the library.

1986   Michael Cross became Director of Leisure (March).

1988   Michael Cross resigned; Vivienne Bennett appointed Museums and Arts Officer
        (January).

1992   Mena Williams retired; succeeded by Judith Farrell (6 July).
        Vivienne Bennett moved to London; Alexandra Walker appointed Museum and Arts
        Officer.

Index